101+ Tricks, Secret Ingredients, and
Easy Recipes for Foolproof Barbecue and Grilling

BIG BOOK OF
BBQ TRICKS

Bill West

Triehouse Publishing

First Edition

ISBN: 978-7356656-3-4

Cover design by 100Covers
Interior design by FormattedBooks

Thank You and a Free Book

Thanks for checking out Big Book of BBQ Tricks. If you like what you see, you'll love my first book "BBQ Sides and Sauces." It's loaded with more photos and recipes from the pages of BarbecueTricks.com. I want to give it to you free just to say thanks for reading.

Download free at
www.barbecuetricks.com/sauces-sides-recipes/

Dedication

My wife, MJ, and I dedicate this book to our Lord and Savior, Jesus Christ

Man shall not live by bread alone.
– Matthew 4:4

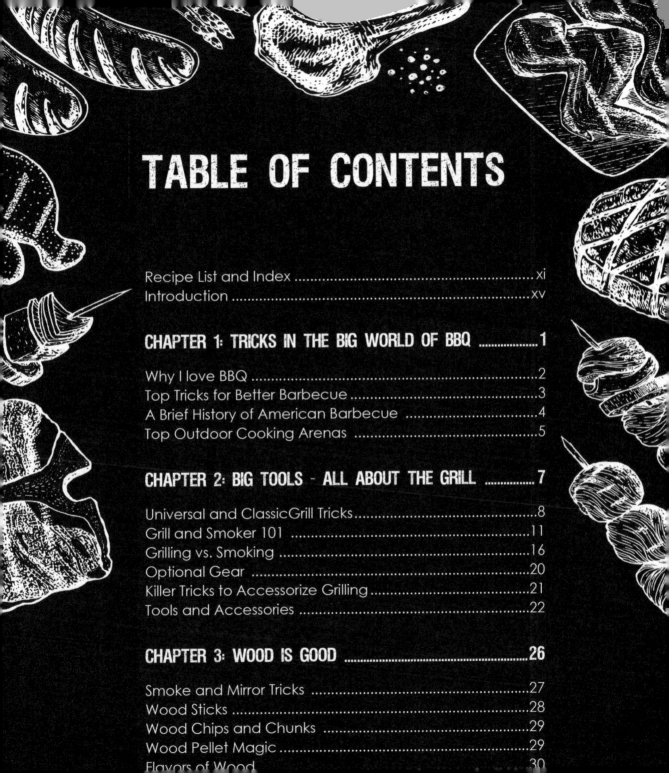

TABLE OF CONTENTS

RECIPE LIST AND INDEX

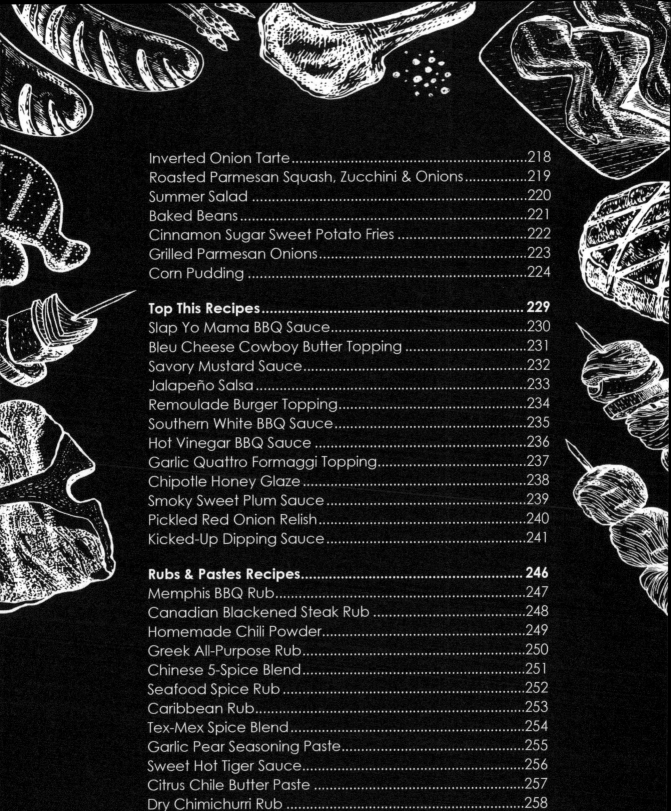

INTRODUCTION

I'm lazy. I am embarrassed to say it, but I love a good short cut or a way to make a challenging job easier. For example, I will gladly use the steam of a hot shower to straighten my clothes if it keeps me from breaking out the ironing board…or I'll spiral cut my hot dog to get more char and condiment gripping surface area. Apologies to barbecue purists, but I'm not too proud to use a microwave to remove silk from corn on the cob (see the trick in Chapter 10)!

I'm the guy who likes to use bar soap as shampoo (then again, I am follicly impaired). You could also say I am cheap. I'm not proud of it, but I like to save a buck. I got that from my father, who relished long day trips to the remote Navy surplus store to take advantage of a good deal.

Those facts, combined with my insatiable love of good food, is why I started BarbecueTricks.com way back in the early 2000s. The internet tsunami was washing over America, and I had a blast sharing juicy photos and YouTube videos as a hobby I could dabble in without the responsibility of it being real work. Shy of a few bucks to own the domain name "BarbecueTricks.com" and blogger tools, YouTube publishing was free! Well, wait…how many spellings are there of barbecue, BBQTricks.com, BarbequeTricks.com…this could get expensive.

The good thing was, it was all about the joy of outdoor cooking, and fun. The problem was, there was not a lot of world wide web organization before hashtags. It's kind of tough to find the right trick when you need it, or to discover the perfect recipe when you're in the hunt.

So I hope you find this book serves as an easy BBQ reference guide. A quick way to find one of the many tips and tricks I discovered along the way as I was in search of a sizzlin' good meal. I thought if I didn't catalog them here, a lot of great tips would just disappear "up in smoke" in the bottomless pit that is the internet.

Each chapter is embedded with a block of the best tricks on each subject, from grills and accessories to spices, and meats. I have also included a handy cheat sheet for finding essential smoking details fast. There is a section on Talking Chop with brilliant barbecue pros, and a few Side Notes to help you match the perfect side dish to your main course. I also tried to keep the classic recipes foolproof and easy to follow (like the 3-2-1 Barbecued Ribs and the Big Beautiful Brisket). A few of these special grills and recipes are tricks in and of themselves, like pellet grills, the Subway Fatty, Ash Kisser T-bone Steaks, or the Grilled Parmesan Onions (recipes in this book). I really hope you enjoy this book.

If you discover just one trick that will make your outdoor cooking easier or saves the life of a child, then it will all be worth it, especially the part about the child.

Last, I want to thank the many readers that have been so kind to take time to review one of my previous books by giving you a free copy of my Sauces and Sides cookbook at https://BarbecueTricks.com/sauces-sides-recipes. Thanks again! Those reviews are deeply appreciated (hint, hint).

So now, if you're hungry for the best in barbecue... let's Fire it UP!

Recipe Key:

= Serves

= Cook Time

= Grill / Smoke / Stove

= Wood

CHAPTER 1

TRICKS IN THE BIG WORLD OF BBQ

"Cooked the pig in the ground, got some beer on ice.
All my rowdy friends are coming over tonight."
—Hank Williams, Jr.

I wrote this book because I really wanted to pull together all the random tricks and tips that have been scattered throughout my website and YouTube videos. There are so many great McNuggets, well, more like riblets, of juicy morsels out there - hard to find, yet delicious on which to nibble. Indeed there are enough true tricks to flesh out each chapter here and even more simple tips I have been able to sprinkle on top. I list out the meatiest tricks where appropriate in each chapter, and spice up other places with tips, as well.

For the opening trick, I simply need to tell you to get creative with your flavors. We all have our favorite flavor profiles. You may like things hot and spicy, or perhaps sweet and tangy. I hereby give you the freedom to experiment and give you permission to fudge on a pinch of this or a spoonful of that. If you are sweating the small stuff, you will miss out on my favorite part about barbecue: the fun. You probably already know what you like. Experiment and trust your gut. If you're like me, you have a lot of gut to work with.

So trick number one is, *have fun*. Although a good magician never reveals his tricks; a good pitmaster always reveals a good time to all.

Why I love BBQ

I have a lot of fun cooking, and cooking outdoors has a long tradition of mixing in laughter, fun, and rowdy good taste. This all started when man said, "What the heck, let's throw it on the fire." It wasn't long after that when he added rustic utensils like sticks and stones to add flare. Then things got really interesting with fat and flare-ups.

The term barbecue is derived from the old Taino Indian word "barbacoa" that translated literally means cooking on sticks over fire or a "frame of sticks." Wood, smoke, fire, and food all come together to define today's general idea of barbecue.

I am writing somewhere along the coast of South Carolina that I have deemed the "birth-place of American barbecue." I say, Christopher Columbus and hungry Spanish settlers experimented with pigs and hot coals somewhere near our Lowcountry Islands and took the first step towards a "pig in the ground and beer on ice." Thank you, Bocephus, for connecting the dots.

The next step was for poverty-stricken Southerners to take the cheap cuts of meat and make them succulent by adding spices, smoke, time, and love. Competition trophies, electric slicers, infrared sear burners, and thousand-dollar Big Green Eggs hatched later.

Today, barbecue rules the airwaves on cooking shows, fast food menus, and what seems like miles of grocery store shelves. However, the true home of barbecue, for me, resides in your own back yard. This is personal.

It's so personal that, to some, the thought of using a trick or short cut is almost blasphemous! They say cutting corners on time and lesser ingredients kill the fun. The time and care eliminated cheats you out of the savoring the moment! I don't entirely disagree but I do know that the fun of experimentation and discovery of new techniques and flavors is part of the fun for me. As the pace of our work life increases, and we approach high-speed information overload, the saving of time is as cherished as our need to slow down. Don't let barbecue become hard work. There is a reason the world's best barbecue joints are only open three or four days a week.

Top Tricks for Better Barbecue

- Start with a clean grill. The black chunks aren't flavor, they're funk. Grab a stiff grill brush and get to work. Remember, a cold grate should never leave grill marks!

- Low and slow is the way to go. Low heat will allow you to slowly break down tough meat fibers and render chewy fat. It also allows more time to be exposed to smoke for another layer of flavor. It does not have to be so for every dish, but to many people, barbecue is defined as Low and Slow.

- Sauce at the end. This way, you avoid steaming the meat, and burning the sugar in sweet sauces that burn before the center of the meat has finished cooking. We'll cover more tasty sauce tricks later.

- Always serve your barbecue hot. It's easier said than done when you cook low and slow, but allow smoked meats to rest while you finish cooking side dishes. Timing is everything. Perfectly heated meats put an exclamation point on more than just one of your senses. The texture and flavor are more succulent on the tongue, the smells are more fragrant, and the sizzle is music to the ears.

- Space out. I don't mean you shouldn't pay attention. I mean give yourself a lot of space on the grill grate. The best trick for avoiding a flare-up is cooking over indirect heat by creating a cool zone on your grill. Strategically place a drip pan beneath fatty cuts. Use the right-sized disposable aluminum pan filled with water. This is especially important with charcoal and wood live fires.

- Smothering flames with a fire-retardant wool blanket is a handy trick. You won't chemically destroy your food in the event of a brief grease flare-up. Char can be good. The blanket can also insulate grills on a cold and windy day. But have a patio fire extinguisher handy just in case.

- Never move a lit grill. Especially not on a trailer. The slightest breeze of air can fuel an ember into a roaring flame. Small pools of oil can become powerful grease fires quickly.

- One of the best tricks to rescue overcooked and tough meat is to slice or chop the portions into an easier to chew format. Too-tough-to-pull pork can be shredded, and razor-thin sliced brisket still packs satisfying flavor with less of a mandible workout. You won't be left to "exJAWstion." Look for more tenderizing tricks in Chapter 6.

- The Gas Hole. In every cookbook I've written, I always preach the rule, "no peeking." The reason is simple. Every time you open the cook chamber, you can add up to fifteen minutes to the total cooking time. My trick for most backyard grills is to leave the lid shut and instead, squint through the gas hole. Seriously, keep it closed as much as you can. If you're looking, you ain't cooking.

A Brief History of American Barbecue

I got my barbecue roots from a somewhat unusual place. I grew up near Chicago, and from my perspective, I was in the center of the food universe. Meat played a big part in my foodie land-scape as Chicago had been considered the country's largest meatpacking center. It was acknowl-edged as the country's meat headquarters in the early 1900s. That's why growing up, I thought I lived in a barbecue Mecca. After all, Weber grills were manufactured and grew to fame from just a few miles away, and ribs and Chicago style hot dogs are a big part of the Chi-town culture. Do you consider hot dogs to be in the barbecue universe? I do. If you agree, let me know your favorite hot dog joint (big or small) by sending me a note (Bill@BarbecueTricks.com). I'd love to know.

I later moved to Peoria for college and discovered hickory smoked rib tips from Big John's Barbecue in Peoria, Illinois, and realized the further south I went, the better the 'cue. Later, when I moved to South Carolina, I discovered mustard sauces and the big world of competition barbecue. That's where I learned there are a lot of regional flavors across the US, and Chicago is best known for pizza and the blues, rather than ribs…still a great place to be.

Here are my directions for where to find America's real barbecue regions.

There are a few targeted areas of the United States that can be considered hot spots for killer barbecue, and they are definitely worth the drive. Some are worth a flight, too.

Cross Country 'Que

o   **The Midwest:** Chicago and Kansas City, with KC being the most commonly regarded as the barbecue Mecca.
o   **The South:** with Carolina mustard style and vinegar sauce, it's all about the humble hog. Pulled pork, whole hog if you can find it, and hash over rice, define the southern style. Memphis is notable as the competition center of America and the home of one of my favorite restaurants, *Charlie Vergos' Rendezvous,* and their dry rub ribs.
o   **Texas:** needs no real explanation as its stellar reputation for beef and serious brisket is legendary. Lockhart and Austin are now tourist destinations on meat merits alone.
o   **California:** has an underrated but very real place on the barbecue map, thanks to the specialized Santa Maria-style Tri-tip that is smoked and traditionally served with pin-quito beans. The triangular-shaped roast from the lower area of the sirloin is hard to find in the East but is deliciously served medium-rare. It's smoked over a live fire utilizing a unique grate that can be actively raised or lowered above the hot red oak coals. Barbecue never looked cooler.

Grillustration: Santa Maria Grill

Top Outdoor Cooking Arenas

There are cooking regions, and there are also barbecue genres that are arenas in and of themselves. Perhaps you fit into one of the following categories of cooking barbecue:

Competition. Competition cooks and judges take their meat very seriously (sometimes too seriously). Braggadocio and trophies are signature signs of this arena, and it is big business. Champions go on to host TV shows, teach expensive classes, and have their own trade groups. The Memphis in May BBQ tournament, and Kansas City Royal are the best-known competitions, but there are other smaller sanctioning groups and big contests in just about every state. In fact, I counted and discovered I could attend a contest somewhere in South Carolina every weekend if I wanted. God Bless 'Merica.

Restaurant. Restaurant dreams live in the hearts of a lot of barbecue enthusiasts. More than a few take the leap, hang a shingle, and open up shop. It's the American dream for many. The food industry has embraced the farm-to-table movement, and that mission fits nicely into this group.

Back-yarders. Backyard aficionados and hobbyists define the silent majority. I'm talking to you if you just like the romance and thrill of the grill. I think I mainly fall in this category, but I love it all. The best part of being a back-yarder is there are no regulations, rules or restrictions. You are not put into a box for the judging of our meats or your selection of the variety of dishes you can dream up on the grill. It's a hobby you can eat! If you are in this group, I think you'll get a lot out of this guide.

CHAPTER 2

BIG TOOLS - ALL ABOUT THE GRILL

"You don't need a silver fork to eat good food."
—Paul Prudohmme

It's kind of weird how the thought of buying a new grill brings out my inner caveman. Maybe it's because fire wrangling is embedded deep down in our DNA. Maybe it's because Tim the Tool Man from Home Improvement comes to mind and triggers my primal grunting responses. Maybe it's because many of today's modern grills and smokers are the modern-day evolution of how to speak in the age-old language of smoke signals.

These unique cooking vessels allow us to harness the power of fire and smoke and magically infuse foods with special flavors and textures that just can't be created in the kitchen.

These cookers, and the cool tools and accessories we use to tame them, are the barrier to entry in the pitmaster club. Some of these grills solve a very specific problem, and others are universally useful. All are beloved in their own way. It's a food problem similar to potato chips. How do you stop at just one?

- **When you buy a new grill, don't skip the burn-in.** Perhaps this should be called the burn-off. It's an hour-long highest heat test run that will help burn off any chemicals, oils, and packaging crumbs that could become toxic smoke. Often new grills will come with instructions on how to season your new toy. If not, you'll still need to run it for at least an hour at its highest heat level before you let it cool again and start with real food. We all love a new grill, but no one likes chicken with a new car smell.

- **My favorite trick for a new grill is to research your hot spots.** Most grills have them, and it can take years to get confident with the areas of the grate that will blast heat more directly than others. One of the first cooks I like to tackle is breakfast. In fact, it's biscuits for all. Start with a few cans (yes, the cheap cans of biscuit dough that come in tubes! I love that, oh so satisfying "thook" you get when popping the tubular cardboard can open. Cover the entire surface of the grill with the raw dough disks, then fire up the grill at its lowest heat and get ready. Bread burns fast, so after a few minutes when you can see or smell the first charring, be prepared to quickly flip each biscuit and keep it on its same spot on the grill grate. Once all are flipped, take a quick photo for future reference. Work quickly and repeat with the other side for confirmation. The clear contrast from white to brown to charred, will be evidence of the hotter areas on the grate. Take another photo and feel free to eat the results. For a sweet version of this, see my **Hot Spot S'mores** *(found in Nuts, Cheese, Desserts & More)*.

- One age-old grill question is this: **Should I cook with the lid of the grill open or closed?** The trick is to judge by the size of the food compared to your hand. If the burger, chop or other meat is thinner than the thickness of your flattened open palm, then you could leave the lid open, but if the meat is thicker than your hand, definitely close the lid and allow for a slower roast.

- **The simple trick for maintaining a clean grill** is to line your drip pans and buckets with aluminum foil to ease clean up. Be sure you don't restrict good air and smoke flow in the process. Or check with your grill manufacturer to see if they sell disposable inserts that serve the same purpose. I love how inexpensive liners help make clean up a snap.

- **Soot busting trouble?** If you cook over a wood fire, you can use my old Boy Scout trick of coating the bottom of pots and pans with a thin layer of dish soap. This protective layer will allow you to rinse away typically stubborn soot that would normally cling to the surface.

- **Make your grill a smoker.** Use this trick to convert your horizontal gas grill into a smoke machine. Create a smoker pouch by wrapping two handfuls of wood chips with heavy-duty aluminum foil and set it next to a burner, or on the coals. I like to start with one handful of chips soaked in water and another dry handful to allow for a longer duration of smoke and smolder. Now, some gas grills come with a built-in smoker box that eliminates the need for a pouch, or you can purchase tubes and smoker boxes (see accessories later in this chapter) that are made to do the same. Place the food to be smoked on the coolest area of the grill, grate away from an active burner or heat source. If you have multiple burners, you should ignite only one and adjust to its lowest setting. Often this is just enough heat to get the wood chips smoking and keep the grill at a low and slow cooking temperature, between 225°F and 250°F. This is why you have that thermometer on the lid! Use it as a way to "see" what's happening inside the grill.

Grillustration: **Making a Gas Grill a Smoker**

- **The easiest technique for cleaning the grill** is similar to how you clean your kitchen oven. Blast it with high heat before and after every cook. Crank it up to the grill's highest setting for five minutes to dry up and burn off all the sticky bits and scrape off any cook surface remnants with a firm grill brush. Some experts suggest placing a sheet of aluminum foil, shiny side down, over the grate to hasten the process. Once you've made this a habit at the end of every grilling session, the "before cooking" routine gets much easier.
- **Zone Out for the best results.** One of the most basic tricks for grilling is to maintain different temperature areas, or "zones," designated across your grate. This will allow you to shift food from one zone to another to avoid flare-ups, fire up a sear, or just hold already

"done" meat until ready to serve. If you are using a gas grill, actually use those front dialing knobs (they have a purpose)! This is the easiest way to create and control your hot and cool zones. For charcoal grills, arrange your briquettes in zero, single, or deeper hot coal layers. A disposable aluminum pan half-filled with water can also help to space your cool zone. It also works great to catch drippings and avoid grease fires.

- **Got gas?** One problem with liquid propane tanks is that it is hard to know how much fuel you have remaining inside. Here is a trick to use before you start your grill. Take a few cups of warm water and pour it slow down the outside of the tank to try to evenly warm its surface from top to bottom. You may need to tilt the tank on a slight angle to make it easier to coat the sides. You can determine the fuel level by touch. The top, empty, part of the tank will stay warm longer. You will feel that the tank is noticeably cooler below the fuel line.

Grillustration: **Tank Level Check**

Grill and Smoker 101

So many Grills…so little backyard. If you're like me, you can only manage the space for two or three grills. Perhaps that's due to budget, patio space, or spousal approval. So you need to make some tough decisions in your hunt. Here's my quick buyers guide to help you navigate.

Kettle Grills - Weber made the kettle grill famous. It was created in the 1950s when a welder at Weber's Metal Works came up with the shape by cutting a metal buoy in half. This is the quintessential American charcoal grill. It's loved for its dependability and predictability. It's very adaptable, and, with a little charcoal wrangling, you can use it for smoking as well as hot and fast grilling. The best part about a kettle grill is simply it's all American nostalgic good looks. They're just cool.

Gas Grills - Gas grills come in different shapes and sizes, but they are typically horizontal ovens. Often stainless steel to minimize rust, with a cart, handles and wheels built-in, they are made to be easily positioned from patio to garage. Though you still shouldn't move a hot gas grill, its portability when cool, is a feature to be considered. Look for a smoker box or small drawer for wood chips and at least two adjustable burners to give you the ability to smoke low and slow. Personally, I like a sear burner and the ability to use a rotisserie, too. This is the easiest kind of grill to use. It's just like an oven. Plus, they can be even more carefree when connected to a residential natural gas line. No more refueling. Alas, if you absolutely must have the flavor of charcoal, gas will not work for you. You probably haven't read this far, anyway.

Eggs - Kamado style grills are charcoal and are typically heavy stone or enamel glazed ceramic material. The Big Green Egg is the big brand name, but there are other manufacturers like Primo. Many of my friends interviewed in the audiobook version of this book (and in the Talking Chop sections forthcoming) swear by them.

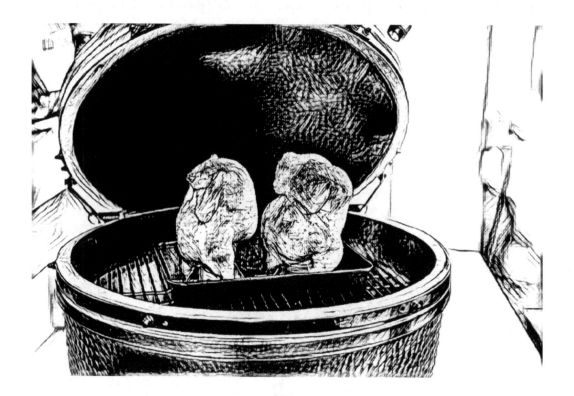

Vertical Smokers - Smokers also have many shapes and the vertical smoker also has many fuel sources. My favorite would be the Backwoods Smoker that runs with a pan of charcoal. Its heavy-duty build quality makes it a favorite of competition cooks. It's really the Cadillac of cookers. My daily driver is a Char-Broil vertical smoker that is electric. I truly believe it is the easiest tool for smoking meat and game. Other options include wood pellet, gas, and wood-burning vertical smokers. One downside to these is that you are restricted to smoking low and slow. There is no hot and fast grilling ability with these smokers.

Bullet Smokers - Charcoal is the primary fuel source for bullet smokers. These pill-shaped smokers are a cross between kettle grills and vertical smokers. In fact, Weber's Smoky Mountain cooker or "WSM" is the gold standard for this type of smoker. Several of our Talking Chop experts use them (see Greg Rempe's thoughts in Talking Chop later in this book). Competition cooks love it for its consistent performance, durability, and lightweight. However, you will need to be ready to commit to stoking wood chips and charcoal for longer duration smoking. One feature I love is the ability to remove the upper portion of the bullet and utilize the lower pan of charcoal to finish off a slow-smoke with a hot and fast "flash" grill over high heat. I started with an electric version of this smoker and still love the affordability of the early Brinkmann models.

Horizontal Smokers - Similar to the shape of a typical gas grill, a horizontal smoker offers a lot of grate space. The horizontal smoker is popular with "stick burner fans." This is when you use split logs in a side firebox as your heat source. The box is positioned on the side to heat the cook chamber indirectly and still provide plenty of flavorful smoke to flow over the meat. A distinct smokestack is also a signature of this smoker, and is popular for competition cooks. Home built versions are sometimes welded out of large steel tanks. They're definitely big boy toys.

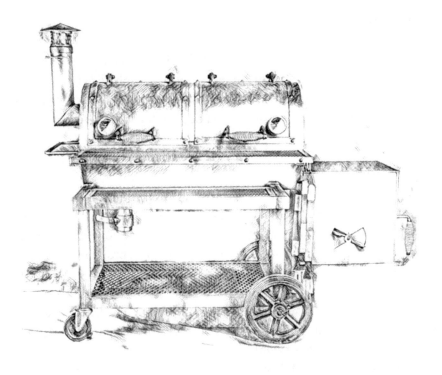

La Caja China - Also known as a Cajun microwave, these rustic wood chests slow cook by inversion. They have been popularized by celebrity chefs like Bobby Flay, and are real conversation starters when cooking for a crowd. In fact, it's hard to cook small portions inside these big, metal lined, wood crates. The heat radiates down from an open pan of charcoal that sits on top of the box. Its inefficient use of fuel is a drawback. They also sit low to the ground, making tending to the coals tough on your back. Plus, the inability to grill and difficulty to clean, make it the worst of both worlds!

Grilling vs. Smoking

If you haven't figured it out already, there is a big difference between smoking and grilling. Both are barbecues, but both types of cooking and cookers are notably different. A smoker is made to hold a low and steady (slow) temperature of approximately 225°F over many hours. Grilling utilizes various temperatures but shines when you need to hit searing hot temperatures suitable for burgers, sausages, chicken, and steaks.

Grilling Is Hot

Using a propane or natural gas grill is sometimes poo-pooed for its lack of showmanship and its lack of wood. In reality, it's the top choice of most American households and should not be underrated. You can achieve championship level barbecue to be proud of with these workhorses of the backyard, but it helps to know a few basic tips, first.

- With a grill, you can make quick work of an evening meal. Once the grill is hot, it's simple to place your meat on the grill, wait four minutes, flip, and repeat. I love going hot and fast without a lot of thinking.
- It all starts by opening the lid. Worth repeating – open the lid – and then you can ignite that satisfying "whoosh" and blue flame. Once the grill is ignited, you can close the lid, but give yourself plenty of time to allow your grill to fully heat up. Charcoal grills do not take long to heat, but I've found my Weber Q and smaller gas grills can take a painfully long time to heat up. You not only need to allow the time to let your grate heat, but often the gas regulators are very sensitive and throttled back for safety. Be patient and give it more time. Once everything is hot, it moves fast. This is where those knobs come into the picture to control the zones. Use them tactically to control cold zones, hot zones, and maybe even a safe zone between. Just because you are grilling doesn't mean you have to forego smoke flavor. Use wood chips, chunks, and smoker pouches to add a layer of smoke flavor as described above.
- It's important for me to insert an additional note about my favorite type of cooker, the Wood Pellet Grill. This magic trick of a cooker is my perfect combination of smoker and grill. I dedicated an entire book – The Ultimate Wood Pellet Grill Smoker Cookbook – to singing its praises. This grill enlists the help of an electric auger to stoke a tiny fire-pot in the bottom of the cook chamber. The size of a teacup, this little fire-pot cranks out more direct heat than you could imagine, and also delivers just the right amount of wood smoke flavor. These grills can pull double duty. Hot and fast, or low and slow, this grill 33handles it without the need to tend a fire. If an electric smoker can be described

as "set it and forget it" cooking, then the wood pellet grill is the next best thing, and you can still pull a rabbit out of your hat with the magic of high heat grilling. Ta daaa!

Grillustration: **Wood Pellet Grill**

Sinking your Teeth into Smoking

I have to admit that when I really think about barbecue, I almost always have smoking in mind. There's no other way to attain the primal succulence of brisket, ribs, and pull apart threads of glorious pork. Smoke is also the secret ingredient in the best barbecue. You can't achieve that glorious bark without it. And it's not just meat that benefits from a lick of smoke. Your vegetables, nuts, and even seafood can be a wonderful blank slate for a fragrant layer of hickory, oak, and applewood smoke.

- You'll need to start with a steady stream of light smoke. Not sooty black smoke but just enough to slowly baste your food. I've heard it described as "blue" in nature, but I've never seen that. Just avoid heavy black smoke that could impart a dirty flavor.

- Take your time with larger cuts of meat. In fact, large pork shoulders and full beef briskets are usually all-day affairs. Constant stoking with wood or charcoal can be fun or work, depending on your mindset. Gas, electric, or Pellet power can alleviate the workload.

- The magic of smoking also derives from the trickery of "low and slow." When you take your time and maintain a temperature range of 225°F to 250°F, something special happens. Meats slowly relax the gelatin and collagen locked up in the fibers to create a new texture. One that is silky, savory, and succulent. If you go too hot, some meat will tighten and get tough; too long and things get dry. Disregard the USDA doneness guidelines and follow the pitmaster's doneness temperatures. Steaks are best served rare, but most smoked barbecue achieves next-level fall-apart tenderness through higher temps.

- Last, cold smoking is also a thing. It's where you're using smoke and spices to cure, rather than cook, your meat – perhaps for jerky. Or you enlist very low temperatures to transmit smoke flavor without the cooking. Aim to maintain a temperature under 100°F, and you can flavor delicate cheeses without melting them. Most smokers struggle to keep the heat this low, so you may need to use a smoker tube or other special cold smoking tool to achieve this special climate inside your cook chamber. A whisp of hickory or mesquite can lift a chunk of boring cheap cheddar to new heights. It's worth the effort.

SMOKING & GRILLING TEMPERATURE GUIDE

Food	Fire	Temp/Time	Target Internal Temperature
Poultry			
Chicken, Whole	Smoke	325ºF, 1½ hours	165ºF
Chicken, Boneless	Grill	Medium-High, 20 minutes	165ºF
Chicken, Cut-Up	Smoke	250ºF, 1½ hours	165ºF
Duck	Smoke	300ºF, 2 hours	165ºF
Turkey, Whole (10-12 lb.)	Smoke	250ºF, 4-6 hours	165ºF
Meat & Game			
Brisket	Smoke	225ºF, 8-10 hours	195ºF-205ºF
Hamburgers	Grill	Medium, 4-5 minutes/side	160ºF
Hot Dogs, All-Beef	Grill	Medium, 5-7 minutes	-
Rack of Lamb	Smoke	225ºF, 4-5 hours	135ºF
Steaks	Grill	High, 5-6 minutes/side	Rare 125ºF Med Rare 135ºF Medium 145ºF Med Well 150ºF Well Done 160ºF
Pork			
Pork Butt, Pulled	Smoke	225ºF, 9-10 hours	205ºF
Pork Chops	Grill	Medium-High, 5-6 minutes/side	145ºF
Pork Tenderloin	Grill	Medium-High, 8 minutes/side	145ºF
Seafood			
Fish	Grill	Medium, 5 minutes/side	145ºF
Salmon	Smoke	200ºF, 1¼-1½ hours	145ºF
Shrimp	Grill	Medium-High, 6 minutes	145ºF
Tuna Steaks	Grill	Medium-High, 3 minutes/side	140ºF

Safety, Troubleshooting, and Maintenance

With all the fun you are having cooking up delicious dishes with your new smoker and grills, you may lose sight of the fact that you are playing with fire - literally. It's time to note a few dangers for which to keep a lookout. Almost half of all home fires are caused by cooking gear. Hot coals from live fire bear obvious risks, but even gas grills need caution.

The National Fire Protection Association says eighty-five percent of grills involved in home fires were fueled by gas, while 10% used charcoal or other solid fuel. Gas grills are involved in an average of 8,700 home fires per year, including 3,600 structural fires and 5,100 outdoor fires annually.

🔥 Be sure to give yourself plenty of room between your grill and everything else. Vinyl siding is the natural-born enemy of a grill. Also, keep your grills clean. Dispose of drippings after every cook and follow these "nevers:"

- Never leave a live fire unattended.
- Never use charcoal on a wood deck or indoors.
- Never wear flip flops while tending hot coals.
- Never transport or attempt to move a hot grill.

But DO, always, keep a dependable fire extinguisher handy.

Optional Gear

I love a good gadget, and if you're into barbecue like I am, I'm sure you have a lot of Cool Tools to choose from. Some are simple, like a good set of tongs. Other items are complex technology, such as digital instant-read thermometers (a must) and computerized Bluetooth "stoker" fans, which scientifically blow oxygen into the smoker box to boost your cook temperature, and are controlled by a digital thermostat.

We'll look closer at some cool tools you'll want in your arsenal in a moment. There are some serious must-haves as well as a few pricey but worth the splurge luxury items. First, a few tricks.

Killer Tricks to Accessorize Grilling

- First off, some of the best things in barbecue are free, like your hands. **When your grill thermometer isn't nearby,** you can always check temperature by "hand." Hover your hand about five inches over the grate and count … one Mississippi… two Mississippi… three Mississippi… ouch! If you must pull away at "one Mississippi," it's considered high heat. After "two Mississippi" that's medium heat. If you can last longer than "three Mississippi" that is considered low heat. It's a handy rule of thumb…or hand, but you can become pretty good at using it as a guide.

- **You don't have to buy expensive grill brushes** for basting. A bunch of natural bristle paintbrushes are friendly on the budget and are perfect for layering thick sauce on meats. Go with small, inexpensive brushes and throw them out when the fibers become difficult to clean. I like the cheap wooden handle brushes from Home Depot.

- **Try silicone basting brushes.** They last forever and are much easier to sanitize and machine wash with ease.

- **Foiled!** A simple roll of heavy-duty aluminum foil can be a pitmaster's best friend. Keep it easy to work with by utilizing those little perforated tabs at the ends of each roll. It's a simple trick I overlooked over decades of awkward roll wrangling.

- **Chill your wrap.** Similarity, plastic wrap also features those same tabs at the end of the box. You can make the wrap even easier to manage by storing the roll in the freezer. Cling wrap, by its nature, clings. The chill will make it temporarily less sticky and easier to handle.

- **Use plastic wrap to back you up when injecting** your next Boston butt. Wrap your roast with plastic tightly. Then, inject with your tasty liquid marinade. The wrap will help hold in your juices while it marinates in the refrigerator. Simply remove the wrap before placing the butt on the smoker.

- **Pizza pans pull double duty.** Save money by choosing inexpensive aluminum pizza screens over pricey grill mats.

- **The trick to searing a steak** in a gas or pellet grill is using a hot cast iron skillet. Get your grill to its highest temperature, and coat the bottom of a cast-iron skillet with a high scorch point oil (see our secret ingredients chapter). Then, fry using the pan's ample surface area to easily brown the flat surface of the steak. What do bears use to cook a steak? A Pan… DUH.

- **More pan handling:** Don't crowd your grill if you're searing meat or sautéing vegetables. Leaving space between pieces allows them to brown and crisp. Crowding leads to soggy, steamed food.

- **Make your cooler even cooler.** Use your old, inexpensive plastic insulated drink cooler as a warming hotbox just like the competition pros, by wrapping butts, brisket, chicken, or ribs, in butcher paper first, and then wrapping in a beach towel, and placing in the cooler to keep warm until ready to serve.

- **That cooler is also a chilly vessel for a brining bucket** when prepping your holiday turkey. It's the perfect size and will help keep the poultry properly and safely chilled.
- **Foiled again!** When you miss a grill brush, a wad of aluminum foil can be a simple problem solver. Grab some sturdy tongs to clamp the foil ball firmly, and scrape the grungy grill grate with it, as you would with a grill brush.
- **You're fired.** A charcoal chimney is great for igniting charcoal, but avoid foul flavored charcoal fluid by lighting with better options like paraffin wax cubes. You can also go old school with just a few sheets of crumpled newspaper. No more newspapers in town? Just use a few sheets cut from the charcoal bag. The dusting of coal will also help keep the bag paper lit.
- **FOILED AGAIN.** No roasting rack for your turkey? Or do you need to raise your butt in your slow cooker or smoker? Fashion a thick ring out of crumpled foil.

As you can see, foil is your friend. I even use it as a heat shield on the grill to keep wooden kebab skewers from burning up.

Tools and Accessories

Must-Have Cool Tools

There are a few items and grilling accessories we all need to have. Use your favorite knives, scoops and spoons. I've long since scored away a dedicated timer thanks to Alexa. And I no longer use a spritz and spray bottle after that ugly Weed-B-Gone accident. Read my "Ultimate Wood Pellet Grill" book for more on that disaster.

I'll share specific brand recommendations on the resources page at BarbecueTricks.com, but here are a few cool tools I think every back-yarder needs handy near the grill.

- **Charcoal Chimneys.** Charcoal purist? You need a Chimney Starter. I think I enjoy the chimney starter more than the actual charcoal. Once you use one, you'll never go back to trying to start a mound of coals again. See my note above on firing them up.
- **Bristle Safe Grill Brushes.** I have come to love the new firm bristle high-heat plastic grill brushes now available. The sturdy bristles are great on the grate, and they won't shed dangerous metal fibers into your food. Plus, because they are made of heat resistant plastic, they are machine washable and won't damage porcelain or ceramic grate coatings.
- **Basting Brushes and Mops.** Like the grill brush mentioned above, I really like brushes that are machine washable. The new silicone basting brushes may feel a bit clinical, but

they make up for the manufactured feel by being easy to sanitize in a dishwasher. Mops do a great job of soaking up a large amount of thin sauces to sop onto meats. More than a few of my YouTube viewers have been aghast at the full-sized Mop that whole hog pitmasters use in my videos. These pitmasters are pros and are using perfectly sanitary mops, albeit big ones for the big meat, like whole hogs, they are handling. You may wish to use the sized drawer models for regular cuts of meat, available for under ten bucks.

- **Meat Thermometers.** You don't have to have a digital version. The good ole analog versions will be ready even if your batteries are not. Go old school and save a few bucks. Just look for one with a gauge that is large enough to read easily.
- **Tongs.** These have to be sturdy and easy to lock or not. Gotta have a few.
- **Meat Tenderizing Mallets.** I use my mallet all the time to prep meat for jerky and to tenderize fajita meat or thick and tough London broil. Stress relief is a nice side benefit. Friendly warning: If you travel with your tools, these will not likely pass through TSA.
- **Grill Grids and Mats.** These flexible mesh or screen sheets are great for smoking small or sticky chunks of barbecue. The screen keeps the pieces from falling through the grate, which helps make clean up easier, and still allows for smoke to surround each morsel of food. Frogmats have become a popular brand to look for, but I say, just pick up some kitchen pizza screens for a few bucks on Amazon. They come in a variety of sizes and clean up nicely in the dishwasher.
- **Smoker Boxes and Tubes.** Sure, you can use heavy-duty foil to create a smoker pouch, but it's nice to have a more durable smoker box or tube to use if you need to add wood this way often. It's easier to handle and the cleanup can be less messy. Go with a steel box that won't corrode too quickly. If you are looking to do some cold smoking or want to add extra smoke to your pellet grill, shop for a smoker tube that's made to use chips or pellets to slowly smolder for hours.
- **Cast Iron Skillets.** Good cast-iron skillets have become useful family heirlooms. Use them to move food from the kitchen oven to the grill and back. They are great for searing steaks or burgers on a pellet grill. Or even as a durable smoker box, similar to the above with wood chips, capped with foil under the grill grate.
- **Grill Basket or Wok.** Sometimes you need to keep smaller items together for grilling. A metal grill basket or grill "wok" can help make fire roasting vegetables easy. We'll use this more in our chapter on vegetables. I love it for quickly grilling marinated zucchini and onions.

Worth The Splurge

A few other items may not be must-haves, but they sure are nice to have. If money is no object or you're into techie gadgets, these goodies are worth the splurge.

- **Quick Read Digital Meat Thermometers.** You don't have to spend over $100 anymore. Just look for something water-resistant. You can find great choices priced from $15 to $90.
- **Digital Remote Thermometers.** You really shouldn't leave your grill unattended too long. But these Bluetooth and hi-tech gadgets with alarms will make you want to challenge that rule. Like the instant-read thermometers, these are priced around $15; but prices vary wildly thanks to advances in small electronics. Remember when handheld calculators were expensive?
- **Electric Meat Slicer.** I really love my Cuisinart brand electric slicer and highly recommend it. But, if you're shopping, it doesn't have to be brand name. Look for a model with a long cord and good grip. If you have brisket in your future, you'll love the way these slicers make quick, clean work out of the largest slabs of tough or tender meat.
- **Stainless Steel Meat Marinade Injectors.** If you plan to do a lot of big meats, you may want to invest in a more durable professional grade marinade injector. I've been able to get by with the plastic freebies that sometimes come with store-bought marinades and turkey kits. However, large models have wider needles that are less prone to spice clogs. It's worth it if you're planning to cook a lot of big meats.

- **Smoking Gun.** This is a tricky little tool to help you add smoke to food that is not cut out for the smoker. It uses food-grade wood sawdust to allow you to add a bit of tactical smoke to smaller items. You can even bubble it through liquids for specialty cocktails and flavorful drinks. Smoky Iced Venti Smokuccino, anyone?
- **Sous Vide and Grill.** The newest tricky technique in barbecue is using a sous vide immersion tool to cook the meat just shy of the perfect internal temperature so you can finish with a quick sear on the grill. My friend Greg Murvich of Ballistic BBQ literally wrote the book on the subject. More on this in Talking Chop with Greg at the end of Chapter 4. Prices vary, but you can usually find a quality immersion cooker for around $100.
- **Bear Claws.** If you cook a lot of pulled pork, bear claws can help ease the process. Bear claws or paws are simple handles with four or five long pointy tines attached to allow you to shred roasts (typically pork) into long strands of meat. There are different models on the market, so beware of cheap plastic models that bend when exposed to heat. Get your Wolverine on!

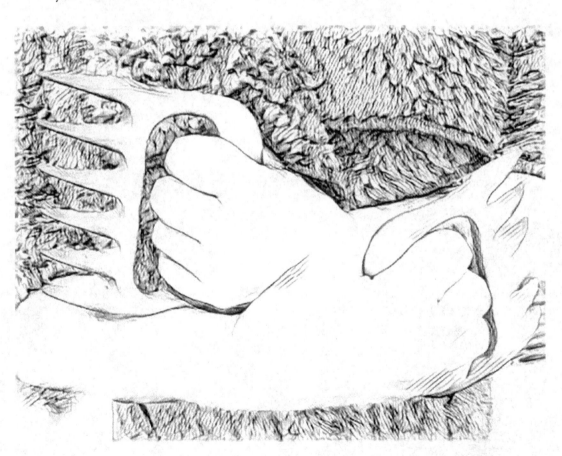

CHAPTER 3

WOOD IS GOOD

*"The ancient wisdom of the Masters says that
even a mighty oak was once a nut like you."*
—Mark Brown

What came first, the wood, smoke, charcoal, or the fire? Whatever your opinion, It ALL came before the chicken or the egg! All that effervescent smoke is the cornerstone of good barbecue. Even the humble hot dog gets elevated to becoming barbecue when it's roasted over live fire. The essence of smoke and meat, I believe, gets burned into the deepest parts of our brain's memory in a unique way. It's visual, it's fragrant, and darned tasty. It uses flavor, sight, smell, and sometimes even sound, to bond with emotions and memories.

And barbecue memories are almost always good. Feasts of the past, you don't just remember, but you savor. Charcoal smoke will always bring me back to my grandfather's house on Sunday evenings, where family gathered around a sizzling Weber grill. The smell of hickory takes me to Mount Pleasant, South Carolina, where I could smell morning smoke from Melvin Bessinger's place down the street when I walked into the radio station most mornings. Applewood makes me think of a warm breakfast with friends at Cracker Barrel. What savor-able memories will you create with one of the wood and smoke varieties in this chapter?

Smoke and Mirror Tricks

- **Jerk.** Looking for a trick to add that authentic Jamaican jerk chicken taste to your meat? Authentic jerk involves pimento wood. It's hard to find most places, but you can emulate it using a blend of oak, and mesquite (a similar hardwood like pimento). Next, create a smoker pouch filled with allspice berries and place it directly under your meat. The fragrant smoke is truly authentic as allspice berries come from the dried unripe berry of Pimenta dioica, a mid-canopy tree, also known as pimento.

- **Foil smoker.** Here's a trick to help you wood-fire salmon without a smoker or cedar planks, by utilizing some aluminum foil and wood chips. Just build a small foil tray and fill it with a bed of wood chips. Set it under the grate, atop the burner or coals, to get the chips smoking. Just like a pouch in the previous chapter, this will add smoky goodness to your fish.

- **Planks for the tip.** Cedar planks made for grilling can be pricey at Whole Foods and other retailers. Instead, grab some untreated cedar shingles at your nearest home store. Make sure it's only cedar (and not chemically treated), and you can snag a bundle for a fraction of the price of the planks at Williams Sonoma.

- **Think local.** Just like farm produce, it's good to use what you can find around the neighborhood. Think local when choosing your smoking woods. If oak is plentiful in your neck of the woods, go with that. Here in South Carolina, pecan is plentiful.

- **Getting' Twiggy with it!** Wooden skewers for kebabs can also flavor your food. Sugar cane sticks can be a sweet choice for fruit kebabs, or if you have a rosemary bush nearby, you can also snag a few green sticks and infuse your kebabs with bonus flavor. Plus, you have a baked-in garnish!

- **To soak or not to soak?** Many pitmasters will advise that you soak your wood chips and chunks to encourage smoldering. Others say it's a waste of time. My trick is a nice compromise. Soak half of your chips and chunks and add both the soaked and unsoaked to the coals in equal amounts. The dry wood will smoke first and the wet will extend the total smolder time.

- **Use what ya got.** Wood pellets that are typically used for your wood pellet grill can also add smoke to you other grills via a smoker pouch or box. Just be careful not to over fill the box. Pellets can expand a bit when heated.

- **Look out for snakes.** Stretch your cook time with a snake. The "snake method" is a trick used by charcoal and kettle lovers. When viewing your grill top from overhead think about it as if it's a clock. You'll line up a row of charcoal briquettes around the circumference of the round charcoal pan from the top of a "clock" on the :00 around to the bottom of the hour, or around :30. Additionally, sprinkle in a generous amount of fragrant hardwood chips at all points between. Start your cook by igniting only one end of the "snake," at the small fire starter cube shown below. You'll enjoy a low and slow smoking heat source from start to finish. Plus, you'll have the added benefit of a controlled safe zone above the drip pan. Last, position your lid's vent holes above the meat for optimal smoke flow.

Grillustration: **Snake Method**

Wood Sticks

If you like to go big, you likely have a big stick burner. This is typically a horizontal offset cooker with a dedicated firebox. The drier, the better. Find a local source for hickory, oak, pecan, or mesquite wood, and get smokin'. To locate a source near you, a Google search usually turns up great prices when you key in firewood. Craigslist or Facebook marketplace are also great places to purchase wood locally.

Wood Chips and Chunks

If you are working with backyard grills, you'll likely be working with wood chips and chunks. I find it is easy to keep these fully stocked year-round, at least in the south. Hickory is almost universally good, but you'll be able to find cherry, oak, mesquite, and applewood at most any Walmart. I recently noticed they keep a wide selection in various sized bags during the spring and summer months. I also keep a current list of exotic wood providers on the resources page at BarbecueTricks.com.

Wood Pellet Magic

Pellet grills are one of my favorite tricks. The compressed sawdust pellets burn cleanly and efficiently. Plus, they can be found in every flavor imaginable. If you are looking for something new, try charcoal pellets. They offer some of the unique characteristics of charcoal and are made specifically for the pellet grill. Mix them with your favorite wood, and proponents claim you'll get a better smoke ring thanks to the higher burn temperature. It's the best of both worlds.

Pellets not only add flavor, but they are also your only heat source, so you'll go through a lot. Expect to burn about a half a pound of pellets for every hour of smoking on your pellet grill's lowest setting. At the highest setting of around 450°F, I've tracked a burn rate of over two pounds an hour. The downside is that pellets can get pricey. Look for sales at the big box stores during the start of summer. The typical price online is a buck a pound, but deals are out there. The best price I've ever seen (and I have been really hunting) is $15 for a 40-pound bag at Lowes on Memorial Day weekend.

Food-Grade Wood Pellets

I've found jaw-dropping prices on pure oak pellets at Tractor Supply. Alas, these pellets are not FDA approved for use in cooking. I have never heard an official reason. The bags say 100% all-natural pure oak. However, a rabbit hole search on the internet has me afraid of getting the bag with a stick of arsenic-laced woodshop scraps. Smoke at your own risk!

{**BONUS TRICK**} One preventable drawback to wood pellets is the large amount of wood dust they can shed. This dust can accumulate in your grill's pellet hopper and be a pain to clean. Instead, seek a clean 12-inch metal soil sieve/sifter, and you can screen out the debris before you reload.

Flavors of Wood

With barbecue wood chunks, pellets, and chips, you can find just about any "flavor" under the sun. Pitmaster blends are typically a blend of hickory and oak. You can also blend endless combinations of your favorites. Here are a few of the best types of wood, and their attributes, for cooking, including a few new VERY unique special flavors of pellets.

WOOD FLAVORS

Acacia	Mesquite family; strong, good for most meats and vegetables
Alder	Delicate with a hint of sweetness; good for fish, pork, poultry, light-meat game birds; great with salmon
Almond	Nutty & sweet smoke flavor, light ash; good with all meats
Apple	Slightly sweet, but dense, fruity smoke flavor; good for beef, poultry, game birds, pork and ham
Apricot	Milder flavor and sweeter than hickory; good on most meats
Ash	Fast burning, light, distinctive flavor; good with fish and red meat
Birch	Medium hardwood with a flavor like maple; good with pork and poultry
Cedar	Used for plank cooking. Typically for salmon or shrimp; try shingles, too
Cherry	Slightly sweet, fruity smoke flavor; good with all meats
Cottonwood	Very subtle in flavor; good on most meats
Grape Vines	Aromatic, similar to fruit woods; good with all meats
Grapefruit	Medium smoke flavor with a hint of fruitiness; excellent with beef, pork, and poultry
Hickory	Pungent, smoky, bacon-like flavor, the most common wood used; good for all smoking, especially pork and ribs – most popular grilling wood in the south
Lemon	Medium smoke flavor with a hint of fruitiness; excellent with beef, pork, and poultry
Lilac	Very light, subtle with a hint of floral; good with seafood and lamb
Maple	Mild smoky, somewhat sweet flavor; good with pork, poultry, cheese, vegetables, and small game birds
Mesquite	Strong, earthy flavor, most meats, especially beef, most vegetables – most popular grilling wood in Texas
Mulberry	Sweet smell and will remind you of Applewood; great for beef, poultry, game birds, pork, and ham

Nectarine	The flavor is milder and sweeter than hickory; good on most meats
Oak	The second most popular wood, heavy smoke flavor, red oak is considered the best by many pitmasters; good with red meat, pork, fish, and heavy game
Orange	Medium smoke flavor with a hint of fruitiness; excellent with beef, pork, and poultry
Peach	Slightly sweet, woodsy flavor; good on most meats
Pear	Slightly sweet, woodsy flavor; poultry, tasty with game birds and pork
Pecan	More like oak than hickory, and not quite as strong; good for most meats, and great for nuts
Pimento	Spicy, similar to mesquite, the wood of the allspice (pimento) berry, which is the choice wood for jerk chicken
Plum	Milder and sweeter than hickory; good on most meats
Post Oak	This Texas oak gets its name from the wood that is used as the popular choice for fence posts. It is, in fact, a distinct species of oak. Very similar to white oak
Walnut	Very heavy smoke flavor, usually mixed with a lighter wood, like Pecan or Apple, and can be bitter if used alone or not aged; good for red meats and game

Blends and Novelty Mixes

I've been surprised by the speed at which companies are creating new flavors and blend options, specifically for wood pellet grills. Here are a few unique pellet options if you like to get more adventurous in your barbecue.

- **How 'Bout Them Apples.** CookinPellets.com offers a wide variety of the basics as well a Black Cherry, and a popular Apple Mash flavor. They'll even ship you a pallet of 15 bags. That is, if your spouse will be okay with parking in the driveway.
- **Got Game?** Traeger has branched out beyond hardware with flavored pellets ranging from an herbaceous Big Game blend for venison, beef, and game, to a rosemary-infused Turkey blend. I like their Leinenkugel's Summer Shandy, featuring lemon zest.
- **All Jacked Up.** Last, Jack Daniels and others sell powerful pellets and wood chips and oak blends made from recycled whiskey barrels. Big meats call for big flavors. I once did a tour of Jack Daniels in Lynchburg, Tennessee, and I highly recommend it. It's like the Willy Wonka factory tour for whisky lovers.

CHAPTER 4

BIG FLAVOR AND SECRET INGREDIENTS

*"I cook with wine. Sometimes I
even add it to the food."*
—W.C. Fields

Variety is the spice of life. However, I think the main spice of barbecue life would be paprika, or perhaps just pepper, or even salt. You'll use plenty of all three. But there is an unlimited mix of herbs, spices, and flavors that can combine to create what we think of as the essence of barbecue. Heck, who doesn't love a "barbecue flavored" potato chip? What spice is that? My friend Kix Brooks of music and "Steak Out" fame says you just need salt, pepper, and good quality beef for a great steak, and I agree. So, although I call some of these "secret ingredients," I really believe it is more the methods and cook times that comprise the "secret." But there are really only a handful of ingredients that can be considered "essentials" for barbecue.

First, know that herbs and spices make up the bulk of this list. So, what's the difference?

Herbs grow. They're leafy (not woody), and in cooking, they don't really like heat. Add herbs at the end.

Spices "like" heat. Typically, spices are bark, seeds, roots, and buds.

Revealing the Secret Ingredients

Did you know famous author Charles Dickens had a legendary spice rack in his grilling kit? It had the best of thymes and the worst of thymes.

Let's take a quick look at some of the best of barbecue herbs and spices.

My Top Ten with a few tricks blended in:

- Allspice. It's got it "all." This is the key to jerk seasoning, AKA the pimento berry
- Celery Salt or Celery Seed. This is nature's curing salt. Many of today's "all natural" sausages and cured meats feature celery for their naturally occurring nitrates.
- Chili Powder. Make your own for the best flavor. More in my chapter, *Rubs and Pastes*.
- Mustard. There are countless varieties of this tiny seed out. The most common are yellow, brown, and black. I'll typically use basic dry mustard in seasoning throughout this book. With sauces, I choose the inexpensive yellow, ballpark variety, table mustard, unless otherwise noted in a specific recipe. I'll almost always coat large meats with it to act as a simple adherent for spices. You use a lot for an adherent, but don't worry. The mustard flavor disappears during a long smoke.
- Pepper: black, and white. Different strokes for different chefs. For best flavor, grind your own from fresh peppercorns.
- Salt. It's all just sodium, right? Yes and no. The shape and size of each crystal give you a lot of options. I lean on coarse kosher salt in this book unless otherwise noted, and because of the larger grain size of kosher salt, it is actually less salt in the recipe, so it is not interchangeable with table salt 1 to 1 in a recipe—more on salt below.
- Tender Quick, AKA Fab. Tender Quick is Morton's brand of curing salt that is imperative for preserving and pickling. It's a mix of salt and sodium nitrite and you can use it to bring out that pink color in meats like enhancing your smoke ring.
- Turbinado Sugar, AKA Sugar In The Raw (see below)
- Vinegar. For centuries this acidic liquid has been used to preserve and flavor food. In barbecue, it adds that tang that compliments fatty meats and rich sauces. I like apple cider vinegar for cooking and clear distilled white or malt vinegar for cleaning.
- Worcestershire. Say it five times fast and you still won't be confident in your pronunciation!

Secret Ingredient Tricks

Sugar and Spice. Sugar can be used in so many different forms, and it has been vilified in the last decade or so. If you are cooking for a competition, it is a well-known secret that "judges like sweet." I'll also say that all forms of sweetener are not created equal (no pun intended). White refined sugar can be replaced by brown sugar in many rubs and sauces for a deeper, less processed flavor, but Turbinado sugar (AKA Sugar In The Raw) is loved by pitmasters because it is a less processed form of crystalized sugar that stands up to heat better than other forms of sugar. Plus, its large crystals add a welcoming texture to robust rubs. Demerara is a similar, English, version of this sugar with even larger crystals.

One big trick to remember is that sugars, notably in rubs and sweet sauces, are best added at the end of high heat grilling. Lower smoking temperatures of 250°F or so shouldn't burn sugars, but use caution. The burning point (called scorch point) of sugar is just above 330°F/165°C.

Salt Basics. Salt also gets a bad rap from today's dietitians, but it is essential to bring out the flavors in great barbecue. Use coarse kosher salt for its consistently large grains. Sea salt is loaded with natural minerals and can have large crystals perfectly suited for hand-ground steak rubs.

When measuring salt, be aware of the designation of table salt or coarse kosher salt. The larger, fluffier, grains of coarse kosher will make it a bit less potent than table salt in equal measure.

- 1 tablespoon of table salt = 1 tablespoon + ¾ teaspoon of coarse kosher salt.
- 1 cup of table salt = 1 cup + ¼ cup of coarse kosher salt

A Course in Coarse. Coarse dry ingredients like coriander, allspice, dry minced onion, peppercorn, and garlic work best for the rustic rubs we'll cover in our final chapter. Plus, toasting and hand grinding any of these will add power to your barbecue.

Vinegar. Dieticians say that vinegar added to your diet will lower your glucose response when you've had a spike in carbohydrates. I'll take it. But the real reason pitmasters use vinegar is for the acidic tang it gives sauces. As a barbecue trick, it's also a great all-natural cleaner. Use it to freshen up your cutting boards with a rubdown and overnight rest before rinsing. Or give your grill grates an overnight bath in a tub of vinegar and a bit of hot water and washing soda crystals. Rinse, dry, and get cooking.

Grease Is The Word. Bacon grease is one of those special ingredients I think of whenever I talk about secret ingredients. It's a tricky fat source I like to use to add a special kick to my **Quick**

Southern Potato Salad *(found in Side Notes)*. Reserve it for later whenever you fry up your next batch of what I call "nature's duct tape". It brings big flavor to boring veggies, too.

The Pro Pitmaster's Pantry

These ingredients may not be in the top ten but are often used by the best outdoor cooks to build big flavors:

- Basil. Add this fresh herb at the end of cooking for fresh results.
- Bouillon Powder/Cubes. This is the secret ingredient to the **Grilled Parmesan Onions** *(found in **Side Notes**)*.
- Cajun Seasoning. It's my all in one choice. I challenge you to try to use Tony Chachere's brand without sneezing.
- Cayenne Pepper. I love the heat. You'll know you used enough when someone asks for a glass of milk.
- Coffee. Use the new microground instant coffee packets, like Starbucks Via. It's great (without the grit) in rubs.
- Coriander AKA Cilantro Seed. The legendary Rendezvous restaurant in Memphis inspired me to add it to the rub for ribs in Chapter 5.
- Crushed Red Pepper. A little bit goes a long way.
- Cumin. A must for Mexican flair.
- Garlic Powder. Use caution to differentiate from Garlic Salt.
- Ginger. It's typically used dry in barbecue, but fresh ginger lasts a long time and adds great flavor to marinades.
- Sweet and Smoked Paprika. Paprika is the base for most barbecue rubs. The best comes from Hungary.
- Lemon Zest. Good things come in small packages. The smallest amounts of lemon or orange zest will give chicken, fish and seafood a flavor boost. It will also freeze for about six months and still retain its punch.
- Mono Sodium Glutamate, AKA MSG, is a secret ingredient in most of the restaurant foods you know and love. It brings out the umami flavors, but alas has a bad reputation with many.
- Molasses. Use this dense syrup to add depth of flavor as well as mellow sweetness.
- Oil, Grease and Lard. See Smoke Points below.
- Tamarind Concentrate. Sometimes called tamarind paste, this has a similar acidity to lemon juice. Fun fact (a fact you'll never need again in your life): It's also a key ingredient in Worcestershire sauce.

- Onion is one of those multi-purpose ingredients that is both a seasoning and a vegetable! We'll talk, and cry, more about onions in my chapter on vegetables.

Smoke Points of Fats and Oils

Safflower Oil	510°F	265°C
Beef Tallow	400°F	205°C
Canola Oil	400°F	205°C
Butter (Clarified)	400°F	250°C
Grapeseed Oil	390°F	195°C
Lard	370°F	185°C
Chicken Fat (Schmaltz)	375°F	190°C
Coconut Oil	350°F	175°C
Olive Oil (Extra Virgin)	320°F	160°C
Butter	250°F	150°C

Tricks for Herbs and Spices

The colonel would be jealous. We have way more than eleven herbs and spices here, plus the tricks to go with them.

Foiled Again! Use a thin layer of foil to ease cleanup when working with bacteria sensitive foods. It is often hard to keep one hand clean when the canister gets dirty with potentially dangerous bacteria.

Have a pinch in a pinch. Here's another handy trick for spices if you cook while traveling. It's simple to create your own personal portable spice rack. Use a Monday through Friday 7-day pill organizer box to store travel-sized amounts of your favorite spices. You'll always have a bit of your favorites at hand.

Make your garlic more a-PEEL-ing. To easily prep a lot of fresh garlic, you can give it a bath in a bowl of water overnight. The next day the previously stubborn skin will slide right off.

Vampire Trick. If you've found you've used too much garlic in a liquid recipe, there's a trick to soften the blow. Parsley absorbs garlic flavors. Put some parsley in a tea ball and give it a swirl for a few minutes. Remove, and then discard the fouled parsley.

Herb Storage. One trick to extend the life of your fresh herbs is to freeze them for later. Stuff them in the bottom of an ice tray, cover each cell with water, and freeze for later use when your favorites are out of season.

Herb Refrigeration. Use this trick to store leafy fresh herbs in the fridge for three to five days. Store herbs like cilantro, by first removing just the leaves from the stems. Then place them on a barely moist sheet of paper towel in a single layer. Roll it up, and store in a baggie with most of the air removed. Equally good is to create an herb bouquet and keep stemmed herbs in the refrigerator like flowers. They'll last longer if your place freshly cut stems in a cup of water, then cover in plastic and refrigerate.

Cold Spice. Give stored fresh spices the cold shoulder. I know that I said spices "like" heat at the start of the chapter, but you do not want to store them over your stovetop. That heat drains their flavor. Instead, keep them cool and in the dark. Keep them dry and protected in an air-tight container in your freezer. They'll remain fresh and sheltered from harsh heat and sunlight that would degrade their freshness over time.

Go Gingerly. Fresh ginger root will often dry out before you use it all up. Stretch its life by storing your ginger in the freezer. It will stay fresh and will be firm and easy to grate directly into your next dish.

Bloom for the boom. Blooming your spices in a dry nonstick pan before cooking allows the natural oils to optimize flavors. Heat them gently in the dry pan with no oil. Watch them closely because more delicate dry ingredients can go from bloomed to toasted to burnt in a flash.

Rockin' your spice world. Don't mash your fresh, tender herbs. Use an extra sharp knife and gently chop them using a rocking motion. This will help to avoid bruising the tender vegetation and seeping all the oil and flavor onto the cutting board.

Never settle. Don't settle for watery mustard with this must-have mustard trick. Store your yellow mustard *upside down* to avoid settling, separating and that dreaded yellow water spurt.

Find it fast. My wife, MJ, is my Organizer in Chief. She brilliantly hand-labels the lid tops of all the identical-looking spice jars so we can quickly discern one red cap from another at a glance. It's a great trick for keeping spices organized and easy to find. I can't get myself to alphabetize them. I really ought to do that…tomorrow.

Measurement Conversions

Imperial	Equivalent	Ounces	Metric Volume	Metric Weight
Dash	¼ teaspoon	-	-	-
1½ teaspoons	½ tablespoon	¼ ounce	7.39ml	7.09g
3 teaspoons	1 tablespoon	½ ounce	14.78ml	14.17g
2 tablespoons	1/8 cup	1 ounce	29.57 ml	28.35g
4 tablespoons	¼ cup	2 ounces	59.15ml	56.70g
8 tablespoons	½ cup	4 ounces	118.29ml	113.4g
12 tablespoons	¾ cup	6 ounces	177.44ml	170.10g
1 cup (16 tablespoons)	½ pint	8 ounces	236.59ml	226.80g
2 cups	1 pint	16 ounces	473.18ml	453.59g
4 cups	1 quart	32 ounces	946.35ml	907.18g
4 quarts	16 cups (1 gallon)	128 ounces	3785.4ml	3kg

Talking Chop: Greg Mrvich of Ballistic Barbecue

There are a lot of smart butchers, pitmasters, and barbecue entrepreneurs out there. I decided to talk with a few about their likes, dislikes, and any tricks they have developed over the years. I've added these discussions to cleanse the palate just after the recipes in five chapters of this book. Check out the audiobook version of this book for even more from these eye opening chats.

I always love talking to Greg Mrvich from Ballistic Barbecue. His popular YouTube channel just surpassed 300,000 subscribers and is going strong. I've known Greg for a long time and am pleased to let you know he's got a couple of great books out. One is on American Sauces and the other is on Sous Vide Barbecue. I asked Greg to clue me in on a couple of his special tricks and tips. Here a brief transcript of our chat edited for time and clarity.

BW:
I love your dry aging videos. Is this something anyone can do?

GM:
Oh yeah. I mean, there are products now to make it easy. I'm a big advocate of that. UMAi Dry is a very, very simple product to use and very affordable. Then, of course, you can buy the little dry agers now that you put in your refrigerator. They also, actually, have standalone units, but those are kind of expensive. I like the UMAi Dry bags because of the ease of use. If you use a vacuum sealer, you can do the UMAi Dry. even if you don't have a vacuum sealer. I did a video showing what they call the immersion method. It's actually a Sous vide technique. You immerse the bag in water with the meat in there and the water pushing on the meat presses the air out off of the surface. Then just cinch it at the top and put a zip tie on it.

I think if you want to dip your toes in dry aging, that's definitely the way to start. Then after that, all you need is a refrigerator and patience because it's very time consuming.

BW:
You've dry aged whole briskets before. Is that worthwhile?

GM:
Yes, for sure. Dry age briskets are something you haven't really seen. You know, all the brisket we buy are wet aged, you know they age it in the cryovac. And I wanted to give Dry aging them a shot and I was personally very, very impressed. I found that it was a lot more, you know, when you dry age that beef flavor gets condensed. So it's a lot more flavorful. And also because you're getting rid of so much water through that dry age process. I mean, when you're cooking, you

know, we're trying to evaporate that water out. And so I never hit a stall when I cooked that brisket. I've done two, I think I did a 30 day and a 60 day, a dry aged brisket and both of them were really good. I want to do a 45 day brisket one of these days.

But, I do think it's worth it. Especially with the big prime rib roasts and everything. Because you're giving that meat more value too because if you buy a dry aged steak at the store you're going to be paying like 30 bucks a pound, you know? So, doing it yourself at home, you're creating very, very expensive cuts of beef and you're not paying that price you'd pay at the butcher shop for it.

BW:
You are a burger specialist. Is that something you use when you're grinding your own burgers?

GM:
With the dry age beef you mean? Yeah, you can grind dry age beef. You know, again, use a lot of patience. So there are different levels of flavor with dry aging. A lot of the typical steaks you'll see at a store have been dry aged 28 days. And that's going to give you a lot more tender cut of beef. More tender than it was before it was dry aged because you've got the enzymes that are in there breaking down the tough tissue, which makes it more tender. And then because everything's shrinking, the flavor gets a lot deeper.

Now, when you start getting into the 60 days, 90 days, a hundred days, you're getting more of a funky flavor. Like an earthy kind of a minerally flavor. Yeah. I personally don't like, you know, I would never do a like a big, like a prime rib personally over 60 days because then you're starting to get into that funkiness, which some people really like, I just personally don't.

BW:
Sous Vide is one of those barbecue tricks that you like a lot. Something you did a whole book on. I think it's one of those trends that we'll continue to see more of. Do you use the technique a lot?

GM:
Most of my Sous Vide cooking I do is not on video. You know, I like to take a sirloin, for example, a sirloin steak and you can make sirloin steak, you can give it the texture of filet mignon almost, you know? So that's kinda what I like to do with it. Just take inexpensive cuts and make them taste like an expensive cut just by cooking them into submission. Making them very tender, and then just giving them a really good sear over some hot lump charcoal. That's usually the type of cooking I do with it.

I also like it when I make baloney. I'll cook it and then I'll put the chub in my sous vide to immerse it and then finish it off that way. It's a really good technique. And also, it's very safe because it's pasteurizing the meat. So you're killing off any pathogens that may have survived the curing process.

BW:
Which one of your sous vide barbecue recipes do you like most?

GM:
I really like sous vide brisket, man. You can simply use a little flat. Just buy a flat and then vacuum seal it, drop it in the sous vide, go to work. Then, literally whenever you want, you can finish it off and have good brisket in the smoker for three hours, let it get some good smoke and let that bark develop.

You'd never know that it was sous vide. And yeah, you'll develop a smoke ring, you'll get a little, like I said, that nice bark and it'll be tender. I'll get it out in just three hours with very little work. And that's probably my favorite just because it's so easy.

Again, like all barbecue guys you can relate to this. There's a kind of a spiritual moment when it comes to running your pit and just kind of patiently waiting for the meat to give up. But, you know, when I was working 10 hours a day, it was nice coming home and just pulling it from the sous vide and throwing it in a smoker for a few hours.

BW:
Yeah. You're not alone with that. I haven't jumped into sous vide but that totally interests me. I think it interests a lot of people.

BW:
How many grills do you have right now and which one do you lean on most?

GM:
That's a tough one. I mean, I have, I'm culling the herd. I'll be honest with you. All my grills, I've given away a lot of stuff. I gave away two pellet cookers. I have my Yoder which I love. People ask me what my favorite cooker is and that would be my Lone Star Grills offset, vertical, I have. I love that thing. I mean the main pit is all quarter in steel, and then the whole firebox is half inch steel. It is just a monster, but it breathes so clean. The smoke I get off of that is so clean and once I get it all up, the temp and, you know, let it settle in. It just is so stable with my temperature. I love cooking on that thing. I'll sit out here with a beer and just stare at it.

BW:

What do you use for wood?

GM:

I love cooking on pecan. I think that's my favorite wood. But I use a lot of Hickory as well. Out here our local wood is oak. We have three different types of Oak trees out here and I can get Oak for free, so I love Oak too.

BW:

What do you think about Wagyu? Worth it?

GM:

But you know, that's the whole theory behind Wagyu is they're keeping those animals, the Japanese, you know, they're trying to keep the stress levels down really low. So that they don't get that lactic acid, which kind of damages the taste, you know, and that's kind of what they've embraced with the way they're raising their steer. I like it. It's very rich. If you get a good, A-5, it's extremely rich. You're not going to be able to sit down and eat a whole steak. If I get it, my wife and I split it. And even then, eating half of a ribeye, you may not even eat the whole thing. It's just so rich.

But if you've never tried it, you owe it to yourself to try it. And you know, I like a good piece of Wagyu because it's something unlike any other, it doesn't compare to anything else that we do. It's in a league of its own. The first time I ever ate it, it stimulated this smile reflex the minute I put it in my mouth and gave that first chew. All of a sudden my wife and I were looking at each other. We were just smiling! We were not saying a word. I mean it was so good.

BW:

I'm doing a comparison of Wagyu to prime now on YouTube.

GM:

I'm sure it's going to be great. Yeah. And it's come a long way since the old days, you know, here in the United States, most of what they're doing is crossbreeding the Wagyu with one of the European breeds that we have out here, like the Angus or whatever. I mean, wagyu means Japanese Cow, but they call it American wagyu or something. People get all bent out of shape on the word, you know, saying American Wagyu because if you translate it literally you're saying American Japanese cow, right? I just like to say we're breeding out the American breed. It's becoming more traditional Japanese steer out here with, with each generation. So I think it's kind of exciting.

BW:
What are the best barbecue joints that you've ever visited?

GM:
Louie Mueller's is way up there. It's in Tyler, Texas. I think right now that's my favorite of all the joints I've been to just because it's the type of barbecue that I'm really fond of. I kind of lean towards that. The Texas kind. I love beef. I love my pork. But I think I love beef more so Louie Mueller's really hits the mark with me. I like rendezvous. I liked Interstate in Memphis. There used to be a place, I think it's gone now.

I think it burned down actually in Oklahoma city called the Knotty Pine that I liked. I like the places that are really old. You walk in there and the walls and the ceilings are stained with smoke. That's the type I like.

BW:
All right, let me do some rapid fire questions! What's your favorite cheese?

GM:
Aged cheddar.

BW:
How do you like your steak?

GM:
Medium rare.

BW:
Do you have a favorite chef?

GM:
I like Anthony Bourdain.

BW:
What do you like on your hotdog?

GM:
I like mustard. Chicago style mustard with a, you know, the sports chilies, the relish, a little celery, salt, tomato.

BW:
A single hot dog. Is it a meal or a snack?

GM:
Single hot dogs. A snack.

BW:
What would you say, cooking wise, is your specialty?

GM:
Well, if you ask you people on YouTube would be hamburgers. You asked me, it's probably a steak and brisket.

CHAPTER 5

POULTRY

"To succeed in life you need three things:
A backbone, a wishbone, and a funny bone."
—Reba

Chicken may be the world's most popular meat on the grill for several reasons. First, it's easy to find in almost any market, it's available in the everyday portion sizes you need. Plus, the tender white meat is a blank canvas for a wide range of flavors. You don't need to add much more than a simple rub under the skin. The ample fat in the bird's succulent skin protects and self bastes the tender meat. It's a quick cook but not always easy because each cut is a different size; white and dark meat dries out at different temperatures, and drippings can quickly flare up to create flash grease fires. It's worth the simple challenge because nothing compares to the rush you get when you bite into a perfectly juicy piece.

I love chicken and turkey on the grill because it tastes great and it's affordable. If you like dark meat, there's not a better deal per pound than a family pack of legs and thighs. You can also grill easy knowing that legs and thighs are almost foolproof on the grill. They're hard to dry out. It's the main reason that competition pitmasters use thighs in competition. They'll cook more than enough and cherry-pick the very best to turn in to judges. There's also a ton of variety you can cook up. Roast it whole, do full leg quarters jerk style, glaze it with a sticky sweet sauce, pile the platter high with crispy smoked wings, or go healthy with a lean white chicken breast. I'll even show you a cool trick later in this chapter to smoke fry (or smo-fry) and cook up hot fried chicken that's better than on the stovetop. Chicken and poultry have never tasted better than when you do it on the grill.

Smoke or Grill

Is chicken better smoked or grilled? I think you can have the best of both worlds by including an extra dose of wood smoke to either cooking method. The milder meat you get with poultry lets wood flavors really stand out, and because the smaller pieces cook fairly fast, it's not an all-day affair. Here are a few quick tricks to help you get the most out of your next cookout starring chicken, turkey and other types of poultry.

- My favorite trick for chicken solves the problem of flabby and fatty skin. You can achieve crispy, bite through, deliciously rendered skin by enlisting a dry brine of table or kosher salt. I use this foolproof trick with wings and drumettes all the time, but it also works for the whole bird or any cut. Start by thoroughly blotting the entire surface of every piece dry with a paper towel, and then salting the entire surface of the skin. Refrigerate for a full four hours to allow the meat to air dry. Be sure you don't pack the pieces together too tightly. You'll want as much surface area and space to allow for air to circulate and dry the skin. When you are ready to cook, blot dry the entire surface of each piece again before adding your recipe's dry seasoning but do not rinse. Be sure you wait until the last fifteen minutes of cooking before adding any wet sauces to the meat.
- When it comes to barbecued chicken, pink does not always mean undercooked. More likely, it's leeching bone pigment or just a smoke ring. But if you can't tell for sure, it's always recommended you use an instant-read meat thermometer to ensure the internal temperature of the bird has surpassed the USDA suggested 165°F.
- Another trick for bite through skin is to get surgical. Competition cooks will remove thick thigh skin and then, with a razor blade or sharp filet knife, scrape and trim off the excess thick fat from the inside of the skin. Then, replace and secure the skin on the chicken with a toothpick for additional rendering and crispiness.
- Chicken can be a slippery beast. One simple way to make handling it better is to grab a few pieces of paper towel to help your grip. This is especially important when slicing. It's actually easier, thus safer, when you use a good, sharp knife.
- Let's talk turkey. Turkey can be great to grill or smoke, but its thick skin is impenetrable by seasoning on the surface. Think of it like a wetsuit. I suggest you gently work your fingers up and under the skin as far as you can. Then, use your fingers to rub extra salt and seasonings generously into the breast and thigh meat. I call it getting to poultry third base. You'll still want to season the outside of the skin, but now, you've gotten to the meat of the matter.
- You can also inject turkey and chicken with melted butter and seasoned marinades. One trick to preserve the bird's exterior appearance is to inject from the inside cavity through the rib cage. You'll get moisture and flavor to the same spot in the meat without piercing the skin.
- If you're feeding a crowd for a Thanksgiving feast, it's tempting to go big. Instead of one overwhelming 25-pound behemoth bird, try two twelve pounders. They'll be much easier to handle, they'll cook faster, and you'll have twice the drumsticks. It's a Norman Rockwell meets Instagram moment.

- Similar to the above trick, try your hand at Cornish game hens. They're essentially just small chickens, and they are readily available in most supermarkets. The presentation will make you a grilling rock star… or a Rock Game Hen star. You like personal pan pizzas? This is personal pan poultry.
- When shopping for chicken, choose air-chilled whole chicken over water chilled chicken, as the water chilling dilutes the flavor and makes it harder to brown.
- Like the competition pros. Cup your chicken thighs in a large muffin pan to give them a juicy uniformed shape. The cups will hold them together as well as hold in their juices.
- Save a few bucks the next time you are cooking chicken by purchasing whole birds and butchering into pieces yourself. Avoid the bigger birds, as they are typically older and not as tender. Young chickens and turkeys also tend to be less fatty. If the breast bone still feels a bit pliable, it is likely from a tender, younger bird.
- Spatchcock is the barbecue term for butterflying poultry. The trick allows you to flatten out the entire bird for the benefit of quicker and more even cooking. It's easier than it sounds. Use a sturdy pair of kitchen shears or scissors and, breast side down, cut out the backbone of the bird. Make two clean cuts along each side of the spine for the entire length of the bird. Once removed, you can gently spread open the cavity and look for the triangular and translucent bit of cartilage. Using a sharp knife, split the cartilage to reveal the breast bone underneath. It will allow you to spread the bird to open wider. Flip, and flatten with gentle force from the heel of your hand.

Grillustration: **Spatchcock**

POULTRY RECIPES

Nashville Hot Smo-Fried Chicken Tenders
Charred Duck with Chipotle Honey Glaze
Korean BBQ Chicken Kebabs
Jamaican Jerk Chicken
Slap Yo Mama BBQ Chicken
Fiesta Fajitas
Melt in Your Mouth Chicken
Opa! Roasted Quail
Crispy Cajun Ranch Wings
Rosemary Skewered Chicken
Grilled Turkey Breast
My Chicken Can

Poultry Appetizers

Sesame Glazed Flats & Drumettes
Asian Lettuce Wraps
Pulled Chicken Salad

Nashville Hot Smo-Fried Chicken Tenders

4   40-45 minutes   Smoke   Pecan

Chicken tenders aren't just for kids anymore, and grownups are always searching for ways to have "fried" chicken without actually frying it. This recipe will do the trick. If you want your tenders to be extra crispy, and your smoker can reach higher temperatures, increase the heat to 400°F or above (do not exceed 450°F) during the last 10 minutes of cooking.

The real trick to "Nashville Hot" is in the finishing sauce. Inspired by the Music City's favorites: According to Hattie B's and Prince's Hot Chicken Shack, the lard (such a naughty word) helps make the heat seasoning cling.

For the chicken
1 tablespoon + 2 teaspoons salt, divided
2 pounds chicken tenders
2 eggs
1 cup buttermilk
1 tablespoon hot sauce
2 cups all-purpose flour
2 teaspoons salt
2 teaspoons freshly ground black pepper
1 cup (2 sticks) butter, melted

For the hot finishing sauce
1 cup lard, melted
3 tablespoons cayenne pepper
1 tablespoon firmly packed light brown sugar
1 teaspoon garlic powder
1 teaspoon onion powder
1 teaspoon smoked paprika
1 teaspoon ground white pepper
½ teaspoon salt
Prepared canned or frozen biscuits, for serving
Southern BBQ White Sauce, for serving (*found in* **Top This**)

Fridge Pickles & Peppers, for serving *(found in **Nuts, Cheese, Desserts & More**)*

1. Preheat the smoker to 375°F and add wood.
2. Rub 1 tablespoon of the salt all over the chicken and refrigerate for 1-2 hours.
3. In a medium bowl, beat the eggs and stir in the buttermilk and hot sauce until blended. Set aside.
4. In a separate bowl, mix together the flour, 2 teaspoons salt and black pepper. Set aside.
5. Put the melted butter in a disposable aluminum foil pan with high sides.
6. Dredge, Dip, Dredge: Dredge the chicken tenders in the flour mixture, then dip into the buttermilk, and dredge again in the flour, and put in the pan of butter. Place pan on smoker rack.
7. Smoke the chicken tenders for 25 minutes.
8. Carefully turn the chicken tenders over, reduce the smoker temperature to 325°F, and continue smoking for approximately 20 more minutes.
9. Stir together hot lard, cayenne, brown sugar, garlic, onion powder, paprika, white pepper, and salt to make the hot finishing sauce.
10. Remove chicken from the heat when a digital thermometer registers 165°F, baste with the finishing sauce, and serve with biscuits, Southern BBQ White Sauce, and Fridge Pickles & Peppers.

 For variety, try the cooked tenders to top mac and cheese, or on top of a garden salad. There, now it's health food.

Charred Duck with Chipotle Honey Glaze

🍗 4　🕐 2 hours　🔥 Smoke　🪵 Cherry

There are so many ways to spell and define BARBECUE. Now I have another. Char Siu, is a Chinese style barbecue. It literally means "fork roasted," and you've probably seen it at your favorite Chinese restaurant prepared using pork and a brilliant red glaze. This version calls for deliciously juicy duck. It will leave you lip smackin' and quackin' for more.

4 duck leg quarters
1 tablespoon **Chinese 5-Spice Blend** (*found in* **Rubs & Pastes**)
1 cup **Chipotle Honey Glaze** (*found in* **Top This**)

1. Preheat and prepare your smoker to hold a steady 300°F, and add enough wood to smoke for 2 hours.
2. Rub Chinese 5-Spice Blend on all sides of duck quarters.
3. Using half the Chipotle Honey Glaze, baste both sides of the duck quarters, and place them directly on the smoker.
4. Smoke the duck for 1 hour.
5. Poke holes in the skin, and using the remaining glaze, baste the duck, and flip pieces over on the smoker rack.
6. Poke holes in the skin on the reverse side and baste before continuing to smoke for approximately 1 additional hour.
7. Remove duck from the heat when a digital thermometer registers 165°F, and serve hot.

 Duck skin is thick and fatty; much more so than chicken. Use your fingers to get some extra rub under the skin and deep into the thigh and leg meat.

Korean BBQ Chicken Kebabs

🍢 10 skewers, serves 6-8   🕐 6-8 minutes per side   Grill

Kebabs make for a spectacular presentation on the grill as well as on the plate. Be sure to mix in more colorful red, yellow and green bell peppers along with the white and red onions. It's like confetti you can eat.

¾ cup soy sauce
¼ cup ketchup
¼ cup firmly packed light brown sugar
¼ cup **Garlic Pear Seasoning Paste** *(found in **Rubs & Pastes**)*
1 tablespoon rice wine vinegar
1 tablespoon sesame oil
1 teaspoon freshly ground black pepper
3 pounds chicken breasts
1 large red onion
1 bell pepper
1 red pepper

1. In a small bowl, stir together soy sauce, brown sugar, Garlic Pear Seasoning Paste, rice wine vinegar, sesame oil, and black pepper.
2. Cut the chicken, onion, bell pepper and red pepper into 2-inch pieces and place into a large bowl.
3. Pour in the soy sauce mixture and stir to coat all pieces well. Let stand for 5 minutes.
4. Preheat the grill to medium-high (350°F - 400°F).
5. Using skewers, thread chicken and vegetables in an alternating fashion.
6. Place skewers directly on the grill grate, and grill for approximately 6-8 minutes per side until charred, and a digital thermometer registers 165°F.
7. Serve hot.

 Foiled again! Use a folded piece of aluminum foil to shield the handle end of your kebab skewers, if wooden. This will help keep them from burning over high heat.

Jamaican Jerk Chicken

🍗 4-6   🕐 1½ Hours   🔥 Smoke   🪵 Mesquite

The Scotch Bonnet pepper is the official pepper of Jamaican Jerk flavor. These stout and kinda cute peppers look like tiny orange lanterns. They'll definitely light you up. I find scotch bonnets difficult to find locally, but the habaneros used here have the same fruity and intense heat. Yeah, mon!

¼ cup corn syrup or cane syrup
8 cloves, whole
3 habanero peppers, sliced
3 tablespoons whole allspice berries or pimento berries, divided
¼ cup chopped green onions
2 tablespoons salt
2 teaspoons cinnamon
2 teaspoons freshly ground black pepper
1 teaspoon cayenne pepper
1 teaspoon cumin
1 teaspoon thyme
8 bone-in chicken thighs
¼ cup olive oil

1. In a blender, combine corn syrup, cloves, habanero peppers, 2 tablespoons allspice berries, green onions, salt, cinnamon, black pepper, cayenne pepper, cumin, and thyme to make a Jamaican Jerk sauce. Blend until the mixture is smooth.
2. Preheat the smoker to 250°F and add wood.
3. Add the remaining allspice berries to the smoker box with the wood.
4. Rub the chicken thighs with the olive oil.
5. Reserving ¼ cup of the sauce for later, then baste the thighs, getting under the skin, as well. Optional: Keep with Jerk tradition and score the legs with three 1" cuts on the top of each thigh.

6. Place the thighs in the smoker and smoke for approximately 1½ hours, until a digital thermometer registers 165°F.
7. Remove chicken from the smoker and baste with the remaining sauce. Serve hot.

 Real cane syrup is a less processed form of syrup you can sometimes find near Aunt Jemima in the grocery store. Use it, or sweet molasses, to give this chicken an added depth of flavor.

Slap Yo Mama BBQ Chicken

🍗 4-6   🕐 9-12 Minutes   🔥 Grill

Barbecue isn't always pretty. There's a reason why some of my favorite barbecue joints have dedicated paper towel rolls at every table. Sometimes you just crave that sticky sweet, messy experience of finger lickin' goodness. This sauced up barbecue chicken satisfies that urge. Just be kind to mama.

3 or 4 teaspoons salt
8 chicken legs
1½ teaspoons freshly ground black pepper
2 cups **Slap Yo Mama BBQ Sauce** *(found in Top This)*, divided

1. Season chicken legs with salt and refrigerate for 1-2 hours.
2. Preheat the grill to medium-high (350°F – 400°F).
3. Remove the chicken from the refrigerator but do not rinse off the salt.
4. Sprinkle pepper on the legs and place them on the grill.
5. Grill the chicken for 2-3 minutes on each of two sides.
6. Put the legs in a disposable foil pan and cover the legs with 1 cup of the sauce.
7. Raise the temperature of the grill to high.
8. Place the pan directly on the rack and grill 5-6 minutes until the sauce is hot and sticky.
9. Remove chicken from the heat when a digital thermometer registers 165°F.
10. Serve hot with remaining sauce.

Loading on a sweet sticky sauce requires you to be on your toes. Typically I leave out the sauce until the end. However the method above gets every inch saucy. If you want some char, finish them with a quick grill over high heat. Just be sure to tend every piece. Flip and move as needed, as char is only a syllable away from being charcoal.

Fiesta Fajitas

🧭 4   🕐 20 minutes   🔥 Grill

Fajitas are more associated with a Mexican meal then American barbecue. But fajitas are great on the grill. The hot and fast heat along with the fragrant smoke from real hardwood will add a deeper flavor then you'll ever attain on the stove top. I spent years as a server in a great Tex Mex restaurant called the Mesa Grill and Cantina and never got tired of serving, or devouring, this sizzling feast.

2 boneless chicken breasts
2 tablespoons olive oil, divided
2 tablespoons **Tex-Mex Spice Blend** *(found in **Rubs & Pastes**)*, divided
2 bell peppers
1 large onion
1 large tomato, diced for serving
1 avocado, sliced for serving
1 cup shredded cheddar cheese, for serving
1 lime, cut in wedges for serving
8 small corn or flour tortillas, for serving
Jalapeno Sauce *(found in **Top This**)*, for serving
Sour cream, for serving

1. Coat the chicken breasts with 1 tablespoon of olive oil and 1 tablespoon of the Tex-Mex Spice Blend.
2. Slice the bell peppers. Slice the onions thick, and separate into large rings.
3. Place cut peppers and onions into a medium bowl and add remaining olive oil and remaining Tex-Mex Spice Blend. Toss until well coated.
4. Preheat the grill to medium-high heat (350°F - 400°F).
5. Place the chicken breasts on the grill for 5-7 minutes per side, until browned and a digital thermometer registers 165°F.
6. Using a grill basket, add in the marinated peppers and onions, and place on the grill beside the chicken. Grill for about 5 minutes, to desired doneness.
7. Slice chicken and plate on a serving platter with peppers, onions, tomato, avocado, cheese, and lime wedges.
8. Wrap tortillas in wax paper or a moist paper towel, and microwave for 30 seconds.

9. Add warm tortillas to the serving platter, and serve immediately with Jalapeño Sauce and sour cream.

 Add a flourish to your presentation by serving your meat and veggies in a sizzling fajita pan. Wear gloves and get the dry pan hot on the fire or stove top, and quickly add a tablespoon of melted butter and then the chicken and vegetables. If you don't have a real fajita pan, a screaming hot cast iron skillet will work just as well. Add a squeeze of lime for a bit of garnish and extra sizzle when serving.

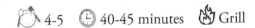

Melt in Your Mouth Chicken

🕑 4-5   ⏱ 40-45 minutes   🔥 Grill

Buttermilk and mayonnaise may seem like a strange combination with chicken. But the unique enzymes in the buttermilk help to tenderize the meat, plus the mayonnaise keeps each piece moist and perfectly coated with spices. It makes each bite just right.

1 whole cut-up chicken
1 quart buttermilk
1 cup mayonnaise
1 cup grated parmesan cheese, divided
6 cloves garlic, minced
2 teaspoons salt
2 teaspoons freshly ground black pepper
1 tablespoon chopped fresh parsley
Garlic Quattro Formaggi Topping *(found in **Top This**)*, for serving

1. Using a large pan or bowl, submerge the chicken pieces in the buttermilk and refrigerate 4 hours or overnight.
2. In a medium bowl, stir together the mayonnaise, half the parmesan cheese, minced garlic, salt and pepper.
3. Preheat the grill to medium-high (350°F - 400°F).
4. Remove the chicken from the liquid and discard the buttermilk, but do not rinse the chicken.
5. Place chicken in a disposable aluminum foil pan with high sides, and coat pieces with the mayonnaise mixture. Sprinkle with remaining parmesan cheese.
6. Place the pan on the grill rack.
7. Grill and bake the pan of chicken about 40-45 minutes until browned and a digital thermometer registers 165°F.
8. Sprinkle chicken with parsley and serve hot with Garlic Quattro Formaggi Topping.

 Load up your plate and serve this with the **Grilled Parmesan Onions** *(found in **Side Notes**).*

Opa! Roasted Quail

🍗 4   🕐 1 Hour   🔥 Smoke   🪵 Apple

I love the creamy, cucumber-fresh flavor of tzatziki sauce. You rarely find it around American barbecue because it's typically paired with gyros or lamb. Here is a good opportunity to include it in a simple smoked quail recipe. It's a delicious way to add some Greek flavor to the grill.

For the tzatziki sauce
1 lemon, juiced
2 cups plain whole milk Greek yogurt
4 garlic cloves, finely minced
1 cucumber, seeded and finely chopped
2 tablespoons finely chopped onion
1 tablespoon chopped fresh dill
1 teaspoon salt
½ teaspoon freshly ground black pepper

For the quail
4 whole quail
2 tablespoons olive oil
3 tablespoons **Greek All-Purpose Rub** *(found in Rubs & Pastes)*
½ cup (1 stick) butter, melted & divided
1 lemon, sliced
2 teaspoons chopped fresh parsley, for serving

1. To make the sauce, in a medium bowl, mix together the lemon juice, yogurt, garlic, cucumber, onion, dill, salt, and pepper until smooth.
2. Refrigerate the sauce until ready to serve.
3. Preheat the smoker to 225°F and add wood.
4. Rub the olive oil over quail and season with Greek All-Purpose Rub on all sides.
5. Place seasoned quail directly on the smoker rack and smoke for 30 minutes.
6. Baste the quail with half of the melted butter and place the lemon slices on top.

7. Continue smoking for about 30 minutes or until the skin is browned and a digital thermometer registers 145°F.
8. Drizzle remaining butter over meat, sprinkle with parsley, and serve with the tzatziki sauce.

 Our Greek All-Purpose Rub is one of those go-to spice blends. Use it on lamb, pork, beef, poultry, or even vegetables. The seasoning is lightly salted and well suited to smoke.

Crispy Cajun Ranch Wings

🍗 3-4   🕐 25-30 minutes   🔥 Grill

Wings used to be considered the cheapest part of the chicken. These days they've become more popular than nuggets, and they are honestly my favorite. From what part of the chicken does the nugget come anyway?

2 pounds whole chicken wings (about 8-10 wings)
2 tablespoons olive oil
2 teaspoons salt
½ cup **Canadian Blackened Steak Rub** *(found in **Rubs & Pastes**)*
¼ cup dry Ranch seasoning
Kicked-Up Dipping Sauce *(found in **Top This**)*, for serving

1. Blot the wings dry with a paper towel and generously sprinkle with salt, on all sides.
2. Place chicken on a baking sheet or in a large dish and refrigerate for a minimum of 4 hours.
3. Preheat the grill to medium-high (350°F).
4. Generously season all sides of the wings with the Canadian Blackened Steak Rub and the dry Ranch seasoning.
5. Blot dry, again, and place whole chicken wings on the grill rack over indirect heat.
6. Grill for 20 minutes, baste lightly with oil and then move the wings to direct heat for 5-10 minutes to char slightly.
7. Remove chicken from the heat when a digital thermometer registers 165°F.
8. Serve hot with Kicked-Up Dipping Sauce.

 You can use the salting trick from the group of tricks earlier in this chapter with smaller wing flats, drummettes, and other full cuts, too.

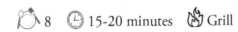

Rosemary Skewered Chicken

🍖 8   🕐 15-20 minutes   🔥 Grill

Sometimes the coolest tricks are the simplest. The beauty of these flashy kebabs comes from the natural look of the rustic and fragrant fresh rosemary twigs.

8 long, sturdy rosemary sprigs
¼ cup olive oil
¼ cup + 1 tablespoon lemon juice, divided
2 teaspoons garlic powder
2 teaspoons onion powder
1 teaspoon dried oregano
1 teaspoon crushed red pepper flakes
2 pounds boneless chicken breasts
1 teaspoon salt
1 teaspoon freshly ground black pepper
1 small onion, cut and separated into small petals

1. Remove the leaves from the bottom half of the rosemary sprigs, mince and place in a medium bowl. Set the sprigs aside.
2. Add the olive oil, ¼ cup of the lemon juice, garlic powder, onion powder, oregano, and red pepper flakes to the minced rosemary and stir until well combined.
3. Reserve ¼ cup of the herb mixture for basting later.
4. Cut the chicken into 2-inch pieces and season with salt and pepper. Add the chicken and onion petals to the bowl of herb mixture and coat well.
5. Thread the chicken onto the rosemary sprigs, alternating with the onion petals.
6. Preheat grill to medium-high (350°F - 400°F).
7. Grill the skewers 10 minutes, turning occasionally.
8. Baste skewers with reserved herb mixture and continue grilling 5-10 more minutes.
9. Remove skewers from the heat when browned and a digital thermometer registers 165°F.
10. Plate the skewers and drizzle with remaining lemon juice to serve.

Keep the tips of your rosemary sprigs from burning by shielding the ends with, you guessed it, a small strip of folded heavy duty aluminum foil.

Grilled Turkey Breast

🕙 8-10   🕐 40-50 minutes   🔥 Grill

I have a buddy that always goes big during the holidays. In fact, when he says "Thanksgiving Turkey and mashed potatoes" he means Wild Turkey and Vodka. This is a lighter take on the traditional bird. People love the breast of turkey because it is such a lean and healthy source of white meat protein. Feel free to go the extra mile for your diet and go skinless... but you can hand off the charred bit of crispy skin to me!

For the brine
1/3 cup salt
1/3 cup brown sugar
2 tablespoons freshly ground pepper
2 quarts water
1 (8-10-pound) turkey breast

For the turkey
2 tablespoons olive oil
1 tablespoon salt
1 tablespoon smoked paprika
2 teaspoons garlic powder
1 teaspoon onion powder
1 teaspoon cayenne pepper
1 teaspoon freshly ground black pepper
1 teaspoon oregano

1. Using a large container large enough to accommodate the turkey breast, add 1/3 cup salt, brown sugar and pepper to the water and stir until dissolved.
2. Submerge the turkey breast in the brine, cover and refrigerate overnight.
3. In a small bowl, stir together 1 tablespoon salt, smoked paprika, garlic powder, onion powder, cayenne pepper, black pepper, and oregano. Set aside.
4. Preheat the grill to medium-high (350°F-400°F).
5. Remove the turkey from the brine and rinse the bird. Discard remaining brine.
6. Pat the turkey dry and apply olive oil all over the breast.
7. Generously rub the bird with the herb mixture.

8. Place the turkey breast on the grill and smoke for 2-2½ hours, until a digital thermometer registers 165°F.

9. Let it rest for 10-15 minutes before carving.

 Serve with the **Roasted Parmesan Squash, Zucchini & Onions** *(found in Side Notes).*

My Chicken Can

 4   1½ hours   Smoke    Hickory

You won't earn your barbecue merit badge until you try your hand at roasting a whole chicken on top of a can of your favorite beer. The brand of beer is irrelevant; it's the added steam from any liquid that helps to keep the meat moist.

Be sure to position your bird and can over a drip pan or a good distance away from direct flame to avoid grease fires.

1 whole (3-5 pound) chicken
¼ cup + 2 tablespoons olive oil, divided
¼ cup **Greek All-Purpose Rub** (*found in* **Rubs & Pastes**)
1 can dark beer
½ cup apple juice

1. Remove the giblets from the cavity of the bird and rub the olive oil all over.
2. Generously apply the rub all over the chicken, under the skin and inside the cavity.
3. Preheat your smoker to a high 325°F and add wood.
4. Drink or discard half the beer and place the opened, half-full can of beer on a flat surface.
5. Carefully place the cavity of the bird over the top of the can and make sure it will stand by itself. Note: propping the legs forward will make it more stable, but you can also purchase a stand for this purpose that holds the can and the bird in place.
6. Gently move the chicken and can onto the smoker rack.
7. Smoke for 1 hour.
8. While smoking stir together apple juice and remaining ¼ cup of olive oil, and place into a clean spray bottle.
9. Spray the bird with half of the apple juice mixture, and continue smoking 30 more minutes.
10. Remove the bird from the heat when browned and a digital thermometer registers 165°F in the thickest part of the thigh.
11. Baste the bird with the remaining juice mixture to finish.
12. With heavy grilling gloves carefully remove the hot can and discard. Carve and serve.

 Don't drink? Replace the beer in beer can chicken with a fresh whole pineapple carved into a stand by trimming (and reserving) the fruit down to the fibrous core and base.

POULTRY APPETIZERS

Sesame Glazed Flats & Drummettes

🍗 4-6   🕐 35 minutes   🔥 Grill

Finger foods like wings are perfect for tailgating. Adding just a pinch of sesame seeds as a garnish right before serving will let your guests know to be prepared for big flavor.

2 pounds chicken flats & drummettes
2 tablespoons olive oil
1 ½ teaspoons salt
1 teaspoon freshly ground black pepper
1 cup **Chipotle Honey Glaze** *(found in* **Top This***)*
2 tablespoons sesame seeds
Pickled Red Onion Relish, *(found in* **Top This***)*, for serving

1. Rub wings with olive oil and salt, including under the skin, and place chicken on a baking sheet or in a large dish.
2. Refrigerate for a minimum of 1-2 hours.
3. Preheat the grill to medium-high (350°F - 400°F).
4. Generously coat the wings with half the Chipotle Honey Glaze.
5. Place wings on the grill rack over indirect heat.
6. Grill for 20 minutes, and then move the wings to direct heat for 5-10 minutes to char slightly.
7. Remove chicken from the heat when a digital thermometer registers 165°F.
8. Baste the wings with the remaining sauce and sprinkle with sesame seeds before serving with Pickled Red Onion Relish.

 Be sure to leave an inch or two of space between each wing to allow for a bit of good heat circulation. Aim to get just a bit of char on every delicious wing.

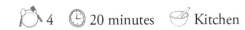

Asian Lettuce Wraps

🍴 4   🕐 20 minutes   🥣 Kitchen

Lettuce wraps are a delicious way in which we cut the carbs at our house. The fresh crunch of the chilled lettuce combined with the spicy hot filling will leave you wanting more. You can't stop with just one.

1 tablespoon sesame oil
1 pound ground chicken
1 medium onion, chopped
1 bell pepper, chopped
3 tablespoons soy sauce
2 tablespoons minced garlic
2 tablespoons Hoisin sauce (or Ponzu)
1 tablespoon rice wine vinegar
1 teaspoon **Chinese 5-Spice Blend** (*found in* **Rubs & Pastes**)
1 teaspoon ground ginger
1 teaspoon freshly ground black pepper
1 teaspoon Sriracha
1 (8-ounce) can water chestnuts, diced
¼ cup chopped green onions
1 head iceberg or butter lettuce, torn into individual leaves

1. On the stove top, in a large saucepan or wok, heat sesame oil over medium-high heat.
2. Add chicken to the pan and cook about 5 minutes until no longer pink.
3. Stir in onion, bell pepper, soy sauce, garlic, Hoisin sauce, rice wine vinegar, Chinese 5-Spice Blend, ginger, black pepper, Sriracha, and water chestnuts, and cook 15 more minutes, until most of the liquid is cooked out. Top with green onions.
4. To serve, spoon 2 tablespoons of the mixture onto a lettuce leaf and fold to eat. Repeat!

🍾 Wash this down with a light and fresh Pilsner. The crispness of the beer and the effervescent bubbles compliment the light and tasty wraps.

Pulled Chicken Salad

 8   🕐 20 minutes   🥣 Kitchen

There are some fancy plastic and metal claws for pulling meat, but a couple of good ol' fashioned forks will do the trick as well. You'll also want to use some heat-resistant gloves to allow you to work with your hands when working with hot meat.

My Chicken Can *(found in Poultry)*, cooked
3 eggs, hard-boiled
½ cup mayonnaise
¾ cup chopped celery
2/3 cup sweet salad cubes (pickles)
¼ cup chicken broth
2 tablespoons sour cream
1 teaspoon salt
1 teaspoon freshly ground black pepper
1 teaspoon celery seed
1 teaspoon garlic powder
Torn lettuce, for serving
Crackers, for serving
Croissants or Sandwich bread, for serving

1. Remove the skin, and debone the chicken.
2. Using 2 forks in a shredding motion, pull the whole chicken and place in a large mixing bowl.
3. Chop the hard-boiled eggs and add to the bowl.
4. Stir in the mayonnaise, celery, salad cubes, chicken broth, sour cream, salt, pepper, celery seed, and garlic powder until well blended.
5. Cover and chill in the refrigerator for a minimum of 1 hour before serving.
6. Serve on a bed of lettuce with crackers, or with sliced bread for sandwiches.

 Work in another serving of vegetables and enjoy this along with the **Cinnamon Sugar Sweet Potato Fries** *(found in Side Notes)*.

Talking Chop: James Peisker of Porter Road

One wise leader in the world of butchery is James Peisker from the renowned Porter Road butchers in Nashville, TN. James co-founded Porter Road and took the company online and national in 2017. He knows his meat.

His advice: Go with quality over quantity. That boost in quality could mean better cuts, dry aging, or even special breeds of animal. Here's our conversation:

JP:

It's not always about the quantity; it's about *the quality* of what you're doing. And it holds true to the backyard barbecue smoker. You don't need to have six pork butts on your smoker! You know, if you're feeding your family and your neighbor and all that, that's a lot!

You know, like doing a brisket, I love smoking briskets. They're big hunks of meat, 10, 12 pounds, you know, I need to line up my friends that I'm feeding. But then I take it, I cut off a piece destined for my slice throughout the week. I cut off the point that is going to go into Chili. That gets wrapped up, that goes into the freezer. I cut off my little bits. Those go back. I will smoke it for more burnt ends. Really make the most of it. Being able to utilize a chicken. Chicken shouldn't be as cheap as it is! Chicken should be something that lives out, it scratches any worms and hangs out with its bird friends, all that good stuff. But a chicken is something that you can make five meals out of for two people.

JP:

That backyard barbecue person is doing all the legwork, but they're often cutting themselves short by buying a cheap piece of meat. And often you go to a big box store and you compare Porter road online to big box store price. Our product is ready for the smoke, it is trimmed up and it's cleaned up. You know, we have that nice quarter-inch, half-inch of fat left on top and it's ready to go. But go to the store, beef tenderloin is the best example. You go to the store for the holiday, you go for beef tenderloin. That Tenderloin you will buy is probably half the price, but you will end up throwing away over half of it, cleaning it up, trimming the scraps, silver skin and all that other stuff off. And then you just wasted all that. All of that stuff will be utilized at our facility for more products, for ground sausage, for all these other things. So it's about making sure that you're shopping consciously because you're doing all the hard work. You're spending the entire afternoon or entire day out by that smoker. Why did you cut the corner when you were sourcing? Why? You can buy a fancy smoker, big old big rig, $2,000 smoker, but you can also use a barrel you repurpose for a hundred dollars. I'd rather spend my money on the meat. The product that goes into it.

BW:

Do the special breeds and cleaner animals change the flavors?

JP:

Yeah. I mean, one of my favorite stories when we first opened the butcher shop in Nashville and we'd have to do a lot of explaining because our prices are more expensive than the grocery store. Because we were paying our farmers correctly, paying the processor correctly. You know, we paid people the way they should be paid, treat people the way they should be treated. But a lady came in and wanted a chicken. It was a little lady on a fixed budget and I wasn't trying to sell her, I was telling her, this is the farm we use. They're out on pasture, they get moved daily, you know, they're fed non-GMO diet. They're raised by one specific farmer and his family of 14, you know, and it's, it sounds like this spiel that I'm doing. But she said, okay, I'm on a fixed budget, I'll try it. And she came back the next day, and she was crying. I was like, "Oh my gosh. What's the matter?" And she said, "I tasted that chicken and it reminded me of my childhood. I haven't had a chicken like that, you know, in over 70 years. And I wanted to thank you." And she's been a customer ever since. We don't see her all the time because she's on that fixed budget. But it's that thing to where food is emotional. Food should be something that brings you together, that is something unique and special.

BW:

Is there any underrated meat out there that you would recommend to a backyarder?

JP:

Yeah, so like if we're going to do like a hidden gem in the backyard smoker for beef, I would say it's a Chuck Roast. Chuck roast is the beef equivalent to a pork butt and it makes this incredible chip beef. Most people think it's only a winter Crock-Pot cut! But you rub that down with a nice, ancho chili, spicy rub to it, smoke it on there, shred it. Man, it makes a mean sandwich.

For pork, we actually had a little fun this year. I always tell my team, "We're not adding more things to the website!" This year we actually *added* pork brisket and pork wings, which are two fun ones that you can't really find. A pork brisket, you know, same muscles, pectoral muscle off a pig. Generally, that piece is cut to the side. It's a picnic cut. But we peeled it back. It smokes in an hour and a half. It's super easy, super delicious. Slice it up. It's amazing! And then that pork wing is the pork shank you whittled down. And then it ends up as this little piece of meat, bone in the middle, and then it's like a little wing. And I smoked those for like an hour, toss them in buffalo wing sauce. Wrap them and throw them back on for another hour. And they're just phenomenal. They're great. They're just fun little pieces.

BW:
Is "bone-in" better?

JP:
Mmm. At times, yes. Bone-in helps protect the meat. It will flavor it ever so slightly. But it is more about protection. Like pork butt, I like bone-in because to get that bone out, you have to butterfly it open. So now you've let all of this place where moisture can go out. But if you leave it together, it's better. So that one in particular, I always think pork butt, and you get the pleasure of like taking out that paddle bone at the end of it! And that's like, I did it!

BW:
How about Wagyu? Is wagyu worth it?

JP:
Wagyu is a breed. It's just like Angus, Berkshire, you know, like all of those things, it can be worth it if it is done correctly. It just depends.

The true Japanese Wagyu where they are in confinement and all that, it's, it's something different. We don't like it because you have to confine the animal to make it marble out that well.

Beef should have fat to it. We prefer that as the American palate. But is too much of a good thing too much?

So… it *can* be worth it to me. But, if I'm going to spend my money, I would probably spend it elsewhere. Like, especially with something like a brisket. You're going to have the juiciest, fattiest, brisket you've ever had. Then you'll be able to eat two ounces, three ounces of it. Yeah, you'll feel it! You know, like at a Japanese restaurant where you're eating a two-ounce slice, I'm all game for it. But beyond that, I think it, it has its novelty purpose and that's kind of it.

BW:
One thing y'all do that's unique is dry aging. Tell me about that.

JP:
Dry aging is something this country used to do exclusively. And then cryovac packing was invented and everyone started doing wet aging.
Beef is a unique animal protein in that it has a natural enzyme found in it and it's not found in pork or chicken. But this natural enzyme remains active in the muscle for six to eight days after slaughter. So that enzyme is continually breaking down and tenderizing the beef. So that's why we always eat beef that is a little aged, whether it's wet-aged or dry-aged. Wet age, means cut up, bagged and put on a shelf, went to a truck that went to a train that

goes to your market. And then maybe a week or so later it's sold to you and they call it "wet aging." That's called shipping to most people!

So, what we do at Porter Road is different. We actually take the entire carcass, hanging, into a humidity and temperature-controlled room. Dry age it, let those enzymes go crazy. But in that process too, we're actually allowing it to evaporate out some of its water moisture, which will concentrate the flavor and make it more delicious. And then, as it's doing that dry-aging process, you're picking up some of those natural flavors in the air. It becomes a very unique, special flavor. Scientists have gotten really good at imitating other flavors, you know, vanilla and things like that. Nobody has ever been able to figure out or pinpoint the flavor compounds that truly make dry age beef what it uniquely is. It's beyond "umami-y" because we can explain umami, you know. We can explain that earthy flavor. But, there is something individually unique to dry age beef that we don't feel that there is ever going to be a reason why we wouldn't do it.

We know that it is economically more expensive for us. It takes more space, it takes more energy, and it obviously gives us less product on the outcome because we're evaporating it out. But we feel like if we will do that and we will continue to be a part of a process, we will make sure it's the best in every step that we do.

BW:
Awesome. What do you grill with at home?

JP:
I am an egg head. I purchased a large, Big Green Egg about 10 years ago and I was a fan of it. And then we started doing food festivals and we got sponsored by a big green egg. And I just, I have become very accustomed to them. I love them. I know how to work with them, but it takes some skill, you know, like it, it's a unique shaped grill. It's a unique grill. I grew up on Weber, you know, the little like $50 Home Depot, Lowe's, Weber that you get. I mean, that's what I smoked my first pork butt on. Like you can do anything in those. It just takes a lot more work and a lot more care. And you know, I love a barrel smoker. I am a charcoal guy. True and true. The most refined I like to go is to a chip. I worked with pellets a long time ago and I personally had never figured out how to make the product I prefer on a pellet smoker. I need to learn from you is what I need to do! I need some lessons from you!

BW:
I love my pellet smoker, but I appreciate all the great aspects of charcoal. I'm relatively lazy and usually in a hurry. So I like to keep it simple. But nothing is cooler than a Big Green Egg and hardwood lump charcoal!

JP:
Oh yeah.

BW:
Rapid fire questions! How do you like your steak?

JP:
Rare.

BW:
What is the best barbecue joint?

JP:
The Gambling Stick. Nashville, Tennessee.

BW:
Your favorite professional chef?

JP:
Thomas Keller.

BW:
What do you like on your hot dog?

JP:
Ketchup.

BW:
Favorite cheese?

JP:
Cabot cloth bound cheddar.

BW:
And last, do you have a specialty at home you cook?

JP:

I guess it would be my sauces. I love a Demi that takes me three days to make. Because, like I said, the more care I put into it, the longer it takes, the more satisfied I am when my friends and family get to enjoy it.

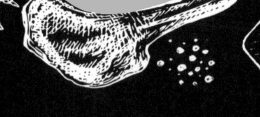

CHAPTER 6

MEAT & GAME

"A hotdog at the ballgame beats roast beef at the Ritz."
—Humphrey Bogart

A wise man once said if God didn't want us to eat animals, He wouldn't have made them out of tasty meat. I agree. I wonder if that wise man was from Texas? Down there, they know that there's nothing quite as satisfying as grilling or smoking a red meat feast on the grill.

The USDA defines "red meat" as "all meats obtained from mammals," but we like to think bigger. Think big cuts of beef, lamb, and even wild game.

Meat plays a starring role in American barbecue. We eat about 25 billion pounds of beef a year in the United States. Believe it or not, per capita, Uruguay and even Argentina actually consume more. Now I see why the new Brazilian steakhouses are so popular. They have the meats!

When you're cooking red meat, you will need plenty of smoke and spice. Think black pepper and mesquite. You'll discover plenty of bold flavors to work with and fire up in the recipes that follow.

Cuts

The most popular beef recipes to cook on a grill have always been hamburgers and hot dogs. I'm definitely a fan; however, there is a much wider variety of beef cuts popular in barbecue. Texas smoked beef brisket is often considered the holy grail of barbecue. Brisket used to be thought of as just an inexpensive, tough cut of meat. But when you smoke it low and slow, it reveals its true colors. When it's good, it will knock your socks off, and when it's bad…well, it's still pretty good.

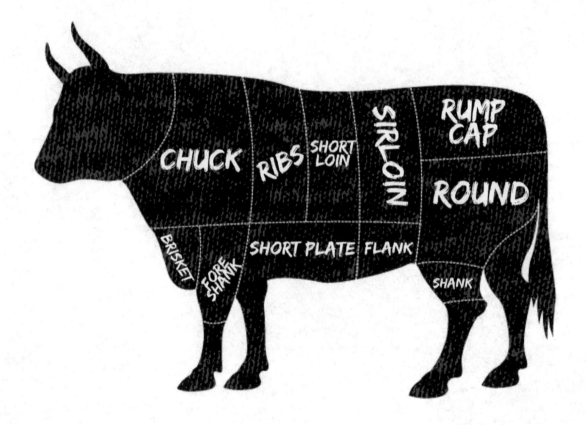

Fred Flintstone sized beef ribs are also a big favorite. The problem with beef ribs is that they can be large, and not everyone has a Texas-sized grill. Beef ribs have a lot of names, but they'll all feature plenty of bone. That's OK. I often say beauty is skin deep, but flavor is to the bone. I think bone-in almost always has better flavor. Yes, bone is a secret ingredient! So, keep the bone in. But in the back yard, you may try a more manageable size. One trick to enjoying the flavor of beef ribs without the bulk is by choosing a streamlined flanken style cut. This cut features multiple bones in a cross-cut strip. Or try the shorter, English style, in 2 or 4-inch segments, featuring one bone each.

Other big beef grilling favorites are the California tri-tip, the massive Texas shoulder clod, thick-cut steaks, and more affordable flank and skirt steaks.

But if you really want to feel like you're eating with the Kings of Game of Thrones, then, a big beef rib is the way to go. However, if it's being served at a wedding, I'd ask for it to go!

Tenderizing Beef

Two more aggressive ways to tenderize tough cuts of beef and game are marinades and meat mallets.

- **Beat it to eat it.** Use a heavy meat mallet on fibrous cuts like flank steak or skirt steak. I promise that starting with a good beating with a mallet will make it easier on your jaw. Plus, the seasoning and char will cook together to resolve any outward appearance of abuse.
- **Great to marinate.** Marinades can contain acids that, with a bit of time, will break down stubborn meat fibers and add seasoning deep into the flesh.
- **Tough it out.** If you're prepping London broil or chewy jerky, you may want to utilize *both* a marinade and the mallet. It's a little more prep that can really give each bite a better chew.

Some cuts of beef require a lot of cooking to help make them tender. There are a few different ways to achieve this. With brisket, stick with a low and slow smoke. This allows the lower temperatures to slowly melt the tough collagen laden tissues in the meat. With brisket, it relaxes into a silky, luxurious, softness once you near an internal temperature of around 200°F. Yes, that's counterintuitive from the USDA recommended doneness temperature of 165°F. But, that's more of a guide for safe consumption of beef, like how rare you can eat steaks safely.

In fact, the USDA guidelines are kind of funny. They also have come up with "grades" of beef that can be confusing. The United States Department of Agriculture labels beef in the following grades, which are nothing more than indicators of fat content.

- **Prime.** This is a rating that means "more inter-muscular fat." It's attached to higher quality meat. Not to be confused with the term "Prime Rib."
- **Choice.** This is typical grocery store quality, but don't be discouraged. It just means "less than Prime." If you can still see ample fat through the packaging, it's probably still a great choice and will be more affordable.

- **Select.** Select is more of a marketing term. Just know it's not as rich as the others. However, it should be cheaper. If you are shopping for leaner meat, it may be what you prefer.
- **Ungraded.** There are also cuts that can still make it to the store. All meat sold in grocery stores is inspected, but it may not be graded. Just be leery of ungraded meat with creative names other than Prime, Choice, and Select.

Grass vs. Grain

Other beef might be labeled grass-fed or finished. Although it has a little different flavor profile, grass-fed beef is prized mainly for its health benefits. It is also considered more humane for the animals. Grass-fed and finished beef comes from cattle that are pasture-raised and fed with only grass, not grain. It's a more expensive process with real dietary benefits. Grass-fed beef has healthy Omega three fatty acids. Also, it is higher in antioxidants, vitamins, and a beneficial fat called conjugated linoleic acid (CLA) that is known for its improved immunity and anti-inflammatory benefits.

Last, I've started to pay attention to hormone-free, organic beef and chicken. I know, when we were kids, *everything* was organic! But I've learned to at least be wary of non-organic meat treated with growth hormones. A new breed of butchers is starting to emerge in the food world. I love a new company called *ButcherBox* that delivers 100 % grass-fed and finished meat direct to your home. They take their meat seriously, and I highly recommend them.

Tricks for Beef, Game, and Lamb

Another smoked cut of meat you will love is Venison. Wait. My autocorrect really wants to give you an "Otter Smoked cut of meat!" I'm thinking that would be gamey.

If you are a hunter or cook meats like lamb and mutton that can drift towards a gamey flavor, there are a few ways to minimize the unusually pungent flavors often found in elk and venison. First, remove all the silver skin and any excess blood. Then, soak the meat overnight in a brine-like solution of either buttermilk or vinegar and water. Below are two simple examples. Remember to use enough to cover the meat completely and discard the liquid afterward. Try mixing these solutions in these ratios:

- One cup vinegar and one tablespoon of salt per quart of cold water
- Or, one tablespoon of salt per quart of buttermilk

Nifty Tricks to Attain the Perfect Bite

- **First, start with a thaw.** Expedite the thawing of meat by utilizing a heavy gauge frying pan. Just fill the pan with hot water and allow it to get warm, not hot. Set the meat in the pan and allow the warm metal to assist in gently drawing out the frost. Repeat and turn the meat a few times, and you will be amazed at how quickly you can get to the next step of your food prep. Heavy copper or aluminum pans work best for this. Avoid solid stainless steel or Teflon pans. However, even they will do the trick upside down, placing the meat on the aluminum core.

- **Better beef equals better flavor.** The premium butcher business has exploded online. You'll pay the price, but it can be worth it. Check my resources page at BarbecueTricks. com for a breakdown on Wagyu. It's a fancy breed of beef loved for its flavorful fat. You could think of it as a grade over and above USDA Prime. Note the difference in American Wagyu and Japanese Wagyu labels. If you can afford the best, I say it's a great trick to enjoy better steak, but not as important for brisket and leaner cuts. If you have the money, you'll love it. We will discuss Wagyu in greater detail in the **Talking Chop** sections later in this book.

- **Hit the right temperature.** Pitmasters target internal temperatures that differ from USDA safety target temperatures. The trick to brisket is that smoked beef brisket internal temperatures need to top over 190°F to be considered tender and "done." The only thing pink with brisket would be the smoke ring. It really needs to get to that higher internal temperature to melt the intramuscular collagen.

- **A handy trick.** Don't have an instant-read thermometer handy? With steak, you can gauge doneness by hand. Relax your right hand. With your left hand's pointer finger, press the pad at the base of your right thumb. This is what "rare" feels like. Now pinch together your right thumb and pinky. When you poke the pad under your thumb, this is what well done feels like. You can gauge your steaks' progress by comparing the firmness with this trick, but, for a truly accurate reading, use a good digital meat thermometer…still, it's handy in a pinch.

Grillustration: **Handy Thermometer**

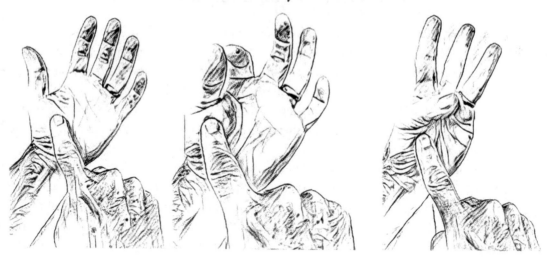

- **Give it a rest.** Beef, like most smoked meat, deserves a good rest. A good rule of thumb is to allow 5 to 10 minutes for steaks, and 15 to 30 minutes for larger roasts. Cutting or slicing too soon will allow more of the savory juices to drain out onto the plate or cutting board. Just let it relax. It'll be difficult to wait, but not too tough…definitely worth the wait.

- **Bone by the pound.** Sure, you can save buying by the pound if you butcher out the bone, but be careful that you're not cutting out the potential flavor. There is a proven, and an undocumented layer of flavor that many say is added when you cook BONE-in. Rodney Scott's secret is to keep in ALL the bones. He insists there is a difference in flavor even when you cook half a hog vs. a whole hog. He points out the spine (and all its surface area) adds its own secret flavor.

- **Don't fear the fat.** If you want big flavor in your beef, you will want some fat. Don't trim it all entirely off your roasts and chops. Leave a half an inch when you can. Also, 80/20 ground beef will make a better burger. 90/10 means that it is 90% lean. It may be healthier, but it's too dry for most.

- **I love a Panade.** You can keep well-done burgers moist by enlisting the help of a "Panade," which is a simple breadcrumb and milk mixture, commonly used for meatloaf. It will coat and lubricate the protein molecules and helps to keep them from binding, shrinking, or getting tough.

- **The Dent.** One famous trick that helps keep thick hamburger patties from balling up is to add a little dent in the center of the raw patty with the tip of your thumb or the end of a spoon. When the meat cooks, the dent will diminish, and you'll have a flatter patty.

- **Grinding your own.** You can grind your own beef for better burgers. Use this trick to kill any possible germs. Drop your ice-cold beef chunks in boiling water for ten seconds immediately prior to grinding. Starting with slightly frozen meat will with grinding, too. The goal is to kill off any possible surface germs, not to fully cook in the boil. Cook immediately after grinding.
- **Sous vide and grill.** Looking to nail a perfect medium-rare every time? Try a handy immersion cooking technique called Sous vide. The technique has been used in the culinary world for years but has recently become a big trick in barbecue. Use the gadget mentioned in our Cool Tools in chapter 2. Sous vide to achieve the perfect internal temperature and then flash finish it on a searing hot grill to achieve the mouthwatering crust and sizzle. More on sous vide in the **Talking Chop** interview later in this book.
- **The reverse sear.** Similarly, you can "reverse sear" and cook thick steaks to perfection with just your grill. Cook "old school" style starting with a low and slow temperature, between 250ºF - 300ºF, over indirect heat. Roast until the internal temperature reaches about ten degrees *below* your final desired internal temp. If you want it around 140ºF for medium (USDA may differ) target 130ºF with a quick read thermometer. Then, pull it off the heat for a few minutes until it just drops slightly. Finally, fire up the grill to direct high heat and sear both sides 1-2 minutes to get a nice charred caramelization and crust. That final step will continue to cook and coax the center of the meat to your perfect finished temperature.
- **Brisket Shortcut**. I know this is controversial, but you can save hardwood, heat, and hassle by finishing your brisket in the oven. You'll need to start with two or three hours on the grill with smoke. At that point, it's absorbed most of its smoke. Once you achieve an internal temperature of 160ºF, wrap it with heavy-duty aluminum foil (AKA the Texas Crutch) and finish slowly in the oven at 225ºF until the brisket has worked its way to a gelatinous and succulent internal temperature of 200ºF. This can be a great trick when you run out of hardwood or fuel.
- **Go against the grain.** Unless you're making jerky, you'll want your red meat to have a tender bite. Help it out by always cutting and slicing your meat against the grain. Note the grain before you season it when you can still see and better discern the lines of the muscle.

Against the grain

MEAT & GAME RECIPES

Big Beautiful Brisket
Bone-in Ribeye
Boneless Leg of Lamb
Backyard Burgers with Pimiento Cheese
Smoky Plum Beef Tenderloin
Chicago-Style Hot Dogs
Tangy Cider Wine Flintstone Ribs
Ash Kisser T-Bone Steaks
Peppered Venison Sausage
London Broil in a Smoky Soy Marinade
Smoked Beef Jerky
Champion Chili

Appetizers

Tomatillo Tacos
Juicy Lamb Shanks
Brisket Sloppy Joe Sliders

Big Beautiful Brisket

🍖 8-12   🕐 8-10 hours   🔥 Smoke   🪵 Oak

Brisket is a feast that will require you to put in a bit of work. But you'll be rewarded with the most satisfying meals of your life. Plan your nap now.

Post oak is the traditional choice for wood to smoke brisket in Texas, so-called because it is also used for fence posts. It's actually a different variety of plant than white oak, but I doubt you can tell the difference.

1 cup salt
1 cup freshly ground black pepper
1 (8-12 pound) brisket
1 cup mustard
1 cup orange juice
1 cup apple juice
½ cup apple cider vinegar
1 cup Slap Yo Mama BBQ Sauce *(found in Top This)*, divided

1. Preheat the smoker to 225°F and add wood.
2. In a small bowl, mix together the salt and pepper. Set aside.
3. Trim off some of the fat from the brisket, leaving about a ½-inch cap of fat for moisture. If the brisket is too large for the smoker, separate the point (or deckle) from the flat to make two roasts.
4. Coat the entire brisket with the mustard and generously apply the salt and pepper all over.
5. Place the brisket in the middle of the rack with the fat side up.
6. Stir together the orange juice, apple juice, apple cider vinegar, and ½ cup of the Slap Yo Mama BBQ Sauce, and pour the "mop sauce" into a clean spray bottle.
7. Smoke the brisket for 4-5 hours until a digital thermometer reaches 165°F.
8. Spray the mop sauce all over the brisket and wrap it tightly in butcher paper or aluminum foil.
9. Place the wrapped brisket back on the smoker rack and continue smoking for 4-5 more hours, spraying with additional mop sauce every other hour.
10. Even if it stalls, leave the meat on until it reaches an internal temperature of 195°F – 205°F.

11. Unwrap the brisket, spray once more with the mop sauce, and let it rest for 45 minutes before slicing.
12. Serve with the remaining Slap Yo Mama BBQ Sauce.

 Many pitmasters make "burnt ends" with the point after smoking. To fix them up, cut the cooked meat into cubes, sprinkle with ¼ cup BBQ rub, glaze them with 1 cup of BBQ sauce and smoke again at 275°F for 1 hour. Yum!

Bone-in Ribeye

🍳 4   🕐 10-12 minutes   🔥 Grill

The ribeye steak is often called the steak lovers steak because it is packed with big juicy flavor that satisfies the pickiest beef eaters. Ribeyes shine thanks to the ample amount of fat embedded in the muscle of the meat. People often brag about the T-Bone and the filet mignon, but in my book, there's nothing that can compete with a ribeye on the grill. It's why The SCA - Steak Cook-off Association (at steakcookoffs.com) mainly use ribeyes. Pull them off the grill before they hit 130°F and let them rest for a medium-rare feast. Look for great marbling and the "tri-heart' at the top of the chops with all three muscles represented.

4 ribeye steaks (about 1½ inch thick)
2 tablespoon olive oil
3 tablespoons **Dry Chimichurri Rub** (*found in **Rubs & Pastes**), divided
1 large red onion
4 ounces (½ stick) butter, melted
½ cup **Bleu Cheese Cowboy Butter Topping** (*found in **Top This**)

1. Allow the steaks to sit out of the refrigerator for an hour to take off the chill.
2. Rub the steaks with olive oil and season with 2 tablespoons of the Dry Chimichurri Rub.
3. Peel the red onion and slice thick, but do not separate the rings.
4. Using metal skewers, thread one of the thick onion slices on each skewer to make onion pops.
5. Drizzle the onions with the melted butter and sprinkle with the remaining Dry Chimichurri Rub. Set aside.
6. Preheat the grill to high.
7. Place the seasoned steaks directly on the grill for 5-6 minutes per side (based on desired doneness) for medium-rare or when a digital thermometer registers a minimum of 130°F, to be considered safe to consume.
8. Immediately top each steak with 2 tablespoons of the Bleu Cheese Cowboy Butter Topping, and let the steaks rest for 5-10 minutes.
9. Place the onion pops on the grill for 2-3 minutes per side. Remove from heat and serve with the steaks.

If you want to really shower your grill with love, fire up a bone-in ribeye or even better, a tomahawk ribeye, which highlights that beautiful rib bone that, as the name implies, resembles the handle of a tomahawk. Thicker, bone-in chops are sometimes called "King Cut" and you can guess why.

Boneless Leg of Lamb

6   4-5 hours   Smoke   Cherry

Lamb isn't quite as popular as other meats in the United States but don't let that keep you from trying your hand at this magnificent cut. Mutton can be found on menus in Kentucky barbecue joints. It's just like lamb but it's from older sheep. Lamb will be more tender and less gamey because it's from sheep younger than one year old. How's this lamb taste? Not baaa-a-a-ad

1 tablespoon garlic, finely minced
2 teaspoons **Homemade Chili Powder** (*found in* ***Rubs & Pastes***)
2 teaspoons kosher salt
1 teaspoon freshly ground black pepper
¼ cup olive oil
1 (5-pound) leg of lamb

1. Preheat the smoker to 225°F and add wood.
2. In a medium bowl, combine garlic, Homemade Chili Powder, salt and pepper.
3. Coat the lamb with olive oil.
4. Apply the rub to the lamb all over, pressing the seasonings into the meat.
5. Place the lamb in the smoker and cook for 4-5 hours.
6. Remove the meat from the heat when a digital thermometer reaches 135°F and let it rest for 15-20 minutes before slicing to serve.

 Cucumber pairs nicely with a generous slice of this lamb. Get your fill by serving this with **Summer Salad** (*found in* ***Side Notes***).

Backyard Burgers with Pimiento Cheese

🍴 6   🕐 8-10 minutes   🔥 Grill

Burgers come in lots of different shapes and sizes. But this monster showcases its southern roots from the top down with a fat dollop of pimiento cheese. It's not just for finger sandwiches anymore!

2 pounds ground beef
1 teaspoon salt
1 teaspoon freshly ground black pepper
1 teaspoon onion powder
6 hamburger buns
2 cups pimiento cheese
6 strips bacon, cooked and cut in half
Fridge Pickles & Peppers (*found in **Nuts, Cheese, Desserts & More***)
Optional toppings: lettuce, sliced tomatoes, onions, mayonnaise, mustard, and ketchup

1. Place the raw ground beef in a medium bowl and season with the salt, pepper, and onion powder.
2. Using your hands, blend well and shape the seasoned meat into 6 thick burger patties.
3. Preheat grill to medium (350°).
4. Grill the burgers for about 4-6 minutes per side (to desired doneness). A digital thermometer should reach a minimum of 160°F to be considered safe to eat.
5. Place each burger on a bottom bun and top with 1/3 cup of pimiento cheese, 1 strip of bacon (cut in half), 1 tablespoon Fridge Pickles & Peppers, plus any other optional toppings. Replace bun top and serve.

Big burgers call for a big paper-plate-bending side dish. Try this one with **Quick Southern Potato Salad** (*found in **Side Notes**).

Smoky Plum Beef Tenderloin

🎇 8-10   🕐 45 minutes   🔥 Smoke   🪵 Mesquite

If you want to splurge for fancy barbecue, look no further than beef tenderloin. It's known to be the cow's most tender cut, thus the name. Unfortunately it's pricey. The tenderloin is a smaller muscle, so it's more in demand from butchers, and you'll pay the price. You'll want to carefully trim off excess fat and all the silver skin with an extra sharp knife. Seasonings won't penetrate too much fat.

1 (5-pound) beef tenderloin
2 tablespoons olive oil
2 tablespoons **Greek All-Purpose Rub** (*found in **Rubs & Pastes***)
Smoky Sweet Plum Sauce (*found in **Top This***), for serving

1. Let the tenderloin sit out on the counter to get the chill off for an hour.
2. Preheat the smoker to 300°F and add wood.
3. Rub the tenderloin with the olive oil and apply the rub all over.
4. Place the meat in the smoker and smoke for 45 minutes until a digital thermometer reaches 130°F.
5. Let the meat rest for 15-20 minutes before slicing to serve with Smoky Sweet Plum Sauce.

 To serve chilled slices instead of hot, refrigerate the smoked tenderloin for 1-2 hours before slicing to serve.

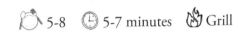

Chicago-Style Hot Dogs

🍴 5-8   🕐 5-7 minutes   🔥 Grill

I'm a hot dog junky, and being from Chicago, this is my favorite way to enjoy a frankfurter. Traditionally "Chicago Style" must include relish, tomato, sport peppers, and celery salt. Go with whatever you like, but, please, no ketchup for me.

8 all-beef hot dogs
4 tablespoons **Savory Mustard Sauce** *(found in **Top This**)*, divided
8 poppy seed buns
8 dill pickle spears
2 tomatoes cut into wedges
½ cup **Pickled Red Onion Relish** *(found in **Top This**)*, chopped
16 sport peppers
2 tablespoons celery salt

1. Preheat grill to medium.
2. Hot dogs are one food that's already cooked so feel free to heat them as you wish.
3. Using 2 tablespoons of the Savory Mustard Sauce, rub each hot dog until well coated.
4. Place hot dogs on the hot grill and cook 5-7 minutes, turning several times.
5. When the hot dogs begin to expand, remove from heat and place in buns.
6. To serve, top each hot dog with a pickle spear, 2 tomato wedges, 1 tablespoon Pickled Red Onion Relish, 2 sport peppers, 1 teaspoon celery salt, and 1 teaspoon Savory Mustard Sauce.

 Since moving to the South I have yet to find "sport peppers" in stores very often. My replacement is the small greenish pickled Tabasco peppers in vinegar. Texas Pete Green Pepper Hot sauce is the most widely available here. You'll have to pop off the shaker top and use a thin fork to get at them.

Tangy Cider Wine Flintstone Ribs

🕐 2-3   ⏱ 4-5 hours   🔥 Smoke   🪵 Oak

Meat tastes better roasted bone-in, and the bones are fun to gnaw. Beef short ribs are a perfect example. I can't think of beef ribs without good ol' Fred Flintstone coming to mind. His giant slab of ribs was so heavy, it tipped over his car! If you cooked the whole rib slab you might look like Fred; however, by definition, beef short ribs are a shortened portion of the entire rib bone. Make them even easier to handle by serving them flanken-style, or English-cut, with the bones cut in 2 or 6-inch lengths. I use a marinade to boost the ribs' natural umami flavors. Umami is the savory in the five basic tastes (sweet, sour, bitter, salty, savory). The addition of beef broth and Worcestershire sauce takes it to the next level, from umami to, "Ooooh, Mommy!"

1 cup red wine
½ cup apple cider vinegar
½ cup beef broth
4 tablespoons **Canadian Blackened Steak Rub** (*found in **Rubs & Pastes***), divided
2 tablespoons olive oil
2 tablespoons Worcestershire sauce
1 tablespoon dry mustard, divided
4 to 6 English-style beef short ribs (about 2 to 2½ pounds)
2 cups apple juice
½ cup **Savory Mustard Sauce** (*found in **Top This***), for serving

1. In a medium bowl, whisk in the wine, vinegar, broth, 2 tablespoons Canadian Blackened Steak Rub, olive oil, Worcestershire sauce, and ½ tablespoon dry mustard.
2. Trim some of the fat off the ribs. Remove the silver skin from the back (thin, white membrane).
3. Place the ribs in a dish and pour the marinade over. Cover and refrigerate for 4 hours.
4. Preheat the smoker to 225°F and add wood.
5. In a small bowl, stir together the remaining Canadian Blackened Steak Rub and the remaining dry mustard, to make a rub.
6. Remove the ribs from the refrigerator and discard the marinade, but do not rinse them.
7. Season the ribs all over with the rub and place them directly on the smoker rack.
8. Pour the apple juice into a clean spray bottle.

9. Smoke the ribs for about 3 hours, quickly spraying them with the apple juice every 30 minutes. This will help keep the ribs moist. Do not leave the smoker lid open long.

10. After 3 hours, remove the ribs from the smoker. Wrap the meat in heavy-duty aluminum foil and spray them with apple juice before tightly sealing the foil.

11. Place the ribs back in the smoker. Smoke the ribs for 1 to 2 more hours, until a digital thermometer registers 200°F to 205°F and the meat is falling off the bone.

12. Remove the ribs from the heat, unwrap, and let them rest for about 10 minutes before serving with Savory Mustard Sauce.

 The membrane on the inside of the rib slab can be difficult to remove. Prior to seasoning the raw meat, use a blunt butter knife to pry up an edge flap of the tough tissue. Grasp with a paper towel and pull or peel off, completely.

Ash Kisser T-Bone Steaks

🍖 4   🕐 35-45 minutes   🔥 Grill

The name here comes from a very primitive way of cooking meat - right on top the hot coals. With the price of beef these days this is not for the squeamish, but it makes for a very macho presentation.

If you are feeling adventurous, use hardwood lump charcoal burned down to white ash and be ready with long tongs, grilling gloves, and a clean natural bristle brush. You'll place these thick chops directly on the hot coals for an almost immediate sear. Give each side 2-3 minutes and then be sure to carefully shake off all the ash and embers before plating. Talk about direct heat!

If that's too intense for you, feel free to take the more conservative (but just as delicious) standard grill approach below.

4 T-bone or porterhouse steaks
2 tablespoons **Canadian Blackened Steak R**ub *(found in **Rubs & Pastes**)*
1/3 cup **Bleu Cheese Cowboy Butter Topping** *(found in **Top This**)*

1. Preheat grill to low.
2. Rub the steaks with the Canadian Blackened Steak Rub.
3. Place steaks on the grill and cook on low for about 30-35 minutes until a digital thermometer reaches 115°F.
4. Increase the grill temperature to high (500°F) and grill each side 2-3 minutes to sear.
5. Cook to desired doneness, and remove from heat when a digital thermometer reaches a minimum of 120°F for safe consumption.
6. Top the steaks with 1tablespoon Bleu Cheese Cowboy Butter Topping, and let the meat rest for 5 minutes before serving. Keep in mind the internal temperature will increase about 5° during that time.

T-bones are not just big in flavor they're big in size. In fact they really are two steaks in one. On one side of the bone you have a delicious piece of tenderloin; on the other, a fatty New York strip - double the fun.

Peppered Venison Sausage

🍖 8-10 🕐 Cure 3 days/Dry 1 hour/Cook 1½-2 hours 🔥 Smoke 🪵 Maple

High in flavor, venison has less fat than beef, so steaks can be tough. It can be prepared in a variety of ways and is best served rare to medium-rare, using dry rubs rather than liquid marinades, which help tenderize it. In this sausage recipe we add some pork sausage to up the fat and cook them all the way to about 170°F. Avoid serving this rare.

3 to 4 pounds ground venison
2½ pounds ground pork
3 tablespoons salt
2 teaspoons Morton's Tender Quick meat cure
2 tablespoons freshly ground black pepper
2 tablespoons sugar
3 teaspoons marjoram
2 teaspoons mustard seed
17 to 30 (3-inch diameter) natural fibrous hog casings

1. In a large bowl, mix together the venison, pork, salt, and meat cure. Refrigerate the meat mixture for 3 days.
2. Add the pepper, sugar, marjoram, and mustard seed to the meat mixture until the ingredients are well incorporated.
3. Stuff the prepared venison into the hog casings. Twist link to link and tie off at the other end.
4. Preheat the smoker to 180°F and add wood.
5. Place the sausages on the smoker rack and smoke them for about 1½ to 2 hours, until the internal temperature registers 160°F on a digital thermometer.
6. Remove the sausages from the heat and serve hot. Or cool and store the sausages in an airtight container in the refrigerator for up to 3 weeks.

Made from hog intestines, most hog casings are simple to stuff, durable, and readily available online. Just be sure to read the package to confirm they're edible, or you'll need to remove the casings prior to eating the sausage. Some casings are plastic, made more for sliced luncheon meat.

London Broil in a Smoky Soy Marinade

🍖 4   🕐 10-12 minutes   🔥 Grill

London broil is more of a style of meat than a cut of beef. In fact, in London they don't really know what you're talking about. Cut your slices thick and be prepared to serve seconds. But bust out the real plates. This main course has some paper-plate-bending heft.

½ cup soy sauce
¼ cup olive oil
2 tablespoons rice wine vinegar
1 tablespoon onion powder
2 teaspoons ground ginger
2 teaspoons dry ground mustard
6 garlic cloves, minced
1 (1½-2-pound) London broil (top round steak)

1. In a small bowl, combine soy sauce, olive oil, rice wine vinegar, onion powder, ginger, mustard, and minced garlic to make a marinade. Set aside.
2. Using a meat mallet, hammer the steak firmly on both sides to tenderize.
3. Place the steak in a shallow dish and cover with the marinade.
4. Place in the refrigerator for 4 hours, turning the steak once, halfway through.
5. Remove the steak from the refrigerator and discard the marinade but do not rinse the meat.
6. Preheat the grill to medium-high heat (350°F-400°F).
7. Place the marinated steak on the rack and grill for 5-6 minutes per side, until a digital thermometer reaches a minimum of 120°F.
8. Remove the meat from the heat and let it rest for 5-10 minutes before slicing to serve.

 If I can't find top round or beef labeled London broil in the supermarket, substitute with a thick flank steak. Sometimes that is easier to find.

Smoked Beef Jerky

Makes 20 slices   4-5 hours   Smoke   Hickory

I'm often shocked at the price of beef jerky in convenience stores. It can get pricey. It's one of the main reasons I make my own at home. I use flank steak here but I'll often simply shop for for the best price on any big and lean steak without a lot of inter muscular connective tissue.

2 pounds flank steak
¼ cup Worcestershire sauce
¼ cup **Tex-Mex Spice Blend** (*found in **Rubs & Pastes***)

1. In a small bowl, whisk together Worcestershire sauce and Tex-Mex Spice Blend.
2. Slice the flank steak against the grain in ¼-inch strips and place into the marinade.
3. Refrigerate 4-6 hours.
4. When ready to beginning smoking, preheat the smoker to 180°F and add wood.
5. Remove the steak from the refrigerator and discard the marinade, but do not rinse the steak.
6. Place the slices on the smoker rack flat and in a single layer.
7. Smoke 4-5 hours until dry.
8. Let cool before serving.
9. Refrigerate any leftovers in an airtight container. Keeps for about 3 weeks, but it won't last that long!

 Pre-tenderize the jerky before you even start marinating. Use a meat mallet and give every inch of the meat a heavy beating. Jerky does not need to be pretty.

Champion Chili

Makes 1½ gallons   2 hours   Stovetop

The secret to award winning chili is not in the meat or beans, it's in the powder. Get the freshest chili powder you can source or, better yet, grind your own.

1 tablespoon olive oil
1 large onion, chopped
1 head garlic, minced
2 pounds ground beef
2 pounds ground pork
1 cup **Homemade Chili Powder** *(found in **Rubs & Pastes**)*, divided
2 tablespoons salt, divided
2 large poblano peppers, chopped
2 (28-ounce) cans crushed tomatoes
2 (15-ounce) cans dark red kidney beans
1 (28-ounce) can diced tomatoes
1 (12-ounce) bottle dark beer
1 tablespoon cayenne pepper
1 tablespoon smoked paprika
1 tablespoon ground cumin
4 chicken bouillon cubes
Shredded cheddar cheese, for serving
Sour cream, for serving
Chopped green onions, for serving
Butter crackers, for serving

1. Sauté chopped onion and garlic in olive oil for 1-2 minutes. Set aside.
2. In a large stock pot on the stove top, over medium heat, brown the ground beef and pork.
3. Stir in ½ cup Homemade Chili Powder and 1tablespoon salt.
4. When the meat is cooked through, reduce heat to low and stir in the poblano peppers, crushed tomatoes, kidney beans, diced tomatoes, beer, cayenne pepper, paprika, cumin, bouillon cubes, remaining Homemade Chili Powder, remaining salt, and onion and garlic mixture.

5. Cover and cook on low for 2 hours, stirring occasionally.
6. Top individual bowls with cheddar cheese, sour cream, and chopped green onions.
7. Serve with crackers.

 The spicy heat of this chili calls for a cold, and bold, beer like a dark lager, IPA, or brown ale.

MEAT & GAME APPETIZERS

Tomatillo Tacos

 6-8   🥣 10 minutes

Taco Tuesday never tasted better. Flank and skirt steak have the best flavor for these tacos. They're not the most tender cuts of beef. Use your meat mallet to soften up the steak before seasoning. Then, after cooking and a rest, slice your flank steak against the grain of the beef for a tender bite.

6 tomatillos, husked and finely chopped
1 medium red onion, finely chopped
½ cup **Sweet Slaw** *(found in **Side Notes**)*
12 soft corn tortillas
2 (1½-pound) skirt steaks
1 cup **Citrus Chile Butter Paste** *(found in **Rubs & Pastes**)*
1 lime, cut in half
¼ cup chopped fresh cilantro

1. In a small bowl, stir together tomatillos, red onion, and Sweet Slaw. Set aside.
2. Preheat the grill to high heat (450°F).
3. Rub the steaks all over with the Citrus Chile Butter Paste and place on the grill.
4. Grill steaks 3-5 minutes per side to desired doneness, but do not remove from the heat until a digital thermometer reaches a minimum of 120°F, for safe consumption.
5. Let the steaks rest for 5-10 minutes before sprinkling with the lime juice and slicing.
6. Wrap corn tortillas in a paper towel or wax paper, and warm in the microwave for 30 seconds. Repeat once, if needed.
7. To serve, fill each tortilla with 3-4 slices of the steak, 2 tablespoons of the tomatillo slaw mixture, and 1 teaspoon cilantro.

 Stick with a south of the border theme and enjoy these tacos with **Mexican Street Corn** *(found in **Side Notes**)*.

Juicy Lamb Shanks

3-4   4-5 hours   Smoke   Hickory

Lamb really benefits from the low and slow cooking powers of a smoker. The long cook breaks down the toughness of this bony cut while the smoke compliments the more gamey flavors inherent to lamb. You'll love it.

6-8 lamb shanks
2 tablespoons olive oil
¼ cup **Canadian Blackened Steak Rub** (*found in **Rubs & Pastes***)
1 cup apple cider vinegar

1. Preheat the smoker to 225°F and add wood.
2. Trim some of the fat and silver skin (the silvery-white membrane) from the shanks.
3. Rub the shanks all over with the olive oil and seasoning.
4. Place the shanks on the smoker rack and smoke them for 1hour without opening the lid.
5. Pour the vinegar into a clean spray bottle.
6. Spray the shanks with the apple cider vinegar and continue smoking for 3-4 more hours, spraying them on both sides every hour, and turning them every other time.
7. Remove the lamb shanks from the heat when the internal temperature registers 190°F on a digital thermometer, and let the meat rest for 10 minutes before serving.

To complete the meal, try serving with **Inverted Onion Tarte** (*found in **Side Notes***).

Brisket Sloppy Joe Sliders

Makes 12 sliders   20 minutes   Stove

Sometimes all you need is a little nibble. This brisket infused classic will help stave off the impatience of your hungriest meat lovers. It's perfect for a top notch tailgate.

2 tablespoons butter
1 onion, diced
1 bell pepper, diced
1 tablespoon minced garlic
1 cup **Savory Mustard Sauce** (*found in* **Top This**)
1 cup **Slap Yo Mama BBQ Sauce** (*found in Top This*)
1½ pounds leftover **Big Beautiful Brisket** (*found in this chapter*), chopped
12 slider buns

1. In a large saucepan over medium-high heat on the stovetop, add the butter, onion, bell pepper and garlic, and sauté until translucent, about 5 minutes.
2. Stir in the Savory Mustard Sauce and the Slap Yo Mama BBQ Sauce, and reduce the heat to low.
3. Cover and simmer the sauce for 10 minutes.
4. Fold in the chopped brisket and simmer for 5 additional minutes before serving warm with the slider buns.

 These sloppy joe sliders are a lot like mini burnt end sandwiches. Wash them down with a fine Pilsner beer straight out of the can.

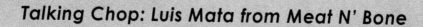

Talking Chop: Luis Mata from Meat N' Bone

Luis Mata is the CEO of a new online meat company called Meat N' Bone. He specializes in premium meats and is based in South Florida.

BW:
What's your most popular product?

LM:
There's not a single product that just stands above the rest. There are some popular ones like the Pinchata, especially the Wagyu. Obviously ribeyes. But it's amazing that it is pretty evenly distributed. Even lesser-known cuts like a Denver steak or flanken style short ribs or flat irons are popular. I think when people have seen the access and the variety, they're willing to try new things.

BW:
I saw you have heritage breed pork. Do you see that catching on at all?

LM:
Yeah, absolutely. I mean, pork is one of our biggest products. We sold a lot of pork. We actually sell some really small suckling pigs. They're about ten pounds, and they're spectacular. Those are very popular with people who like to smoke and do longer cooks. Yeah, Even game meats. Something like elk. I think we've found that niche and there's not a lot of people offering it, and there's not a lot of people offering the quality or having the knowledge to sell the product. So when in our store, when you walk in, it's like buying a luxury watch. If you've ever bought a Rolex, you walk in, we try to do that experience. We actually sit down and talk with you and have a conversation. Meat N' Bone is kind of like old school butcher meets the new world of quick and on demand.

BW:
You're dealing with high-end meats. Is Wagyu worth it for everybody?

LM:
I think it depends. Many people ask me, what's the best? Is it Japanese A-5? And the answer is no, it isn't. There's no best. Best is what you like the best. A-5 is really rich. Some people fall in love with it. To me, my favorite cut is a "cowboy." I use the prime cowboy steak prime ribeye. There's nothing like it. It's a matter of taste.

It is fun seeing the differences. So we sell a ton. We sell choice, which is priced the same as the supermarket all the way up to Japanese Wagyu A-5. We have about 19 different types of ribeyes that we sell. You put them next to each other and you can see the beef, you see the marble and you see the color. When you taste it, there's actually a huge difference between one or the other.

So it's about finding what you like and I think that's the adventure we offer.

BW:
What cuts of beef and pork would you say are underrated that you think people should try?

LM:
So my back-yard guys should always try a picanha, also called a coulotte. It's like a top sirloin, and you leave the fat on. It's incredible. South Americans have been cooking that forever, and it's an amazing price value. From the inexpensive choice all the way to Wagyu. It's spectacular.

Another cut that's coming to prominence is a Denver steak. It's more popular on the West coast, it's an amazing steak and it's a lot cheaper than most cuts. I think the flat iron has started to make some noise. Tri-Tip is another one that everybody should try, especially if you like to smoke.

Even a baseball steak can be pretty good. It comes from the sirloin. It's cut in the shape of a baseball, kind of like a little bit flatter. It's very nice. One thing that we try to do is we offer high-end quality of cheaper cuts. So, for example, a baseball, if you get a baseball USDA choice, obviously it's going to be chewy. It's going to be very beefy. It can be nice, but you have to cook it right. Now, if you grab a baseball steak of Miyazaki A-5, it's spectacular. Its like, "Wow, what is this!?" It's pretty hard to source and procure, and we don't even have a lot of it, but that's where I find the fun.

In terms of pork. I was amazed when I tried the Iberico pork, which is imported and raised from Spain. Acorn-fed. That was insane. Dry age is another thing that's interesting because where you age makes as much of a difference as how you age. A steak aged in Chicago is not going to taste the same as a steak aged in Miami. There's so much to do, there's so much to try.

One of the challenges with Picanha aka Coulotte, with that cut is that it's, it's a whole muscle. So it's a bigger cut. It's about, on the low end is going to be two pounds on the, on the, on the far end could be as much as eight. A Japanese will be 11 pounds, which is massive. So the challenge with it is the quality makes a big difference.

BW:
You have a very clear chart of beef grading on your site. Does the U.S. grading system mean as much as people think it does?

LM:

There are a few things that they'll look at but mostly maturity and it's going to look at the marbling, but that doesn't tell the whole story. So the USDA goes is up as far as prime and that's it. And they'll look at those two factors. When you look at other countries like Australia and Japan, they are similar, but with a lot more detail. But at the end of the day, what I've discovered is what matters is the details, the devil is in the details. The difference between a $50 cowboy steak prime and a $40 cowboy steak prime. It may be how that cattle was fed and how it was raised and how it was cut.

The labeling is a good place to start to look, but there's also a sweet spot on some steaks that are choice that can be almost as good as a prime. Then you're saving the premium. On the flip side, there are some cuts where it's worth going for the prime.

You're judging the whole steer by the ribeye. That doesn't necessarily translate as well to the rest of the animal. So that's where it makes a difference to know the details.

BW:

Is that the case? It's all basically judged out of the ribeye?

LM:

Yeah, like there's other factors, but the biggest driving factor in terms of grading is a marbling on the ribeye. Exactly. On the 13th ribeye, I believe.

BW:

What do you barbecue with at home?

LM:

I am a huge fan of Weber. I find that from a price value perspective, their grills, their smokers, everything. It just lasts forever.

The only thing I would suggest to anybody is if you don't have access to grill, everybody has an oven and it's actually amazing.

Use a cast-iron skillet and a little bit of avocado oil. So your whole apartment doesn't smell.

That's it. You can cook anything in there.

BW:

Any tricks you would share?

LM:

The first thing, use good ingredients. If you talk to any good chef, what you put in is going to have a big impact on what comes out.

Also, I love the South American, especially Argentinian, style of cooking which is slow and low. It's about patience. I like the art of their "asado" where it's a whole day ordeal. Low and slow. So I'd also say have patience.

And the last thing I would say is people use a lot more seasoning than they have to. If you have quality product, for the most part, all you need is salt. Let the beef be the flavor of what you're getting.

BW:
What's the best barbecue joint or steakhouse you've ever been to?

LM:
Green Street Smoked Meats in Chicago. I've been there a couple of times and I thought it was amazing. Definitely, if I had to pick a steakhouse to go to, it would probably be Swift and Sons.

BW:
Both Chicago. My hometown. I need to plan a trip. Do you have a favorite chef?

LM:
Francis Mallmann. He's very interesting. Yeah.

CHAPTER 7

PORK

"I wanted to eat a Pig in a Blanket... In a blanket."
—Kevin Malone

I live in South Carolina where good barbecue means delicious pulled pork. Or if you're really lucky, it's a whole hog pig pickin'. There's so much to choose from. From the ribs to the hams, it's way better than fine dining. It's *swine* dining!

Smoking a juicy Boston butt is one of the simple pleasures of barbecue. When you do it right, the end result will be mounds of pulled and succulent meat fibers piled high on your plate. Bread and buns are optional. If you nail it, the sauce can be optional on the side, too. You wouldn't serve a hamburger without a bun, but good pulled pork with bits of salty, savory bark dotted in the mix, can stand alone as the main course. It's that glorious.

Plus, because you'll be smoking for hours, it will give your family plenty of time to use the line, "Oooh, your butt smells terrific."

Pork is my top choice for everyday barbecue, not just because of the variety from ribs to chops, but also because of the price. Beef and brisket can be budget busters. However, I can always afford a fast cooking pork chop. It never disappoints.

Cuts

There a lot of cuts to choose from between the rooter and the tooter. Ribs, bacon, pork chops, tenderloins, and more bacon, never fail to delight on the grill.

Most cuts of pork are readily available in all supermarkets and most are great on the grill. If you have the time, go low and slow with a pork shoulder. If you're working hot and fast, a bone-in pork chop may be the best choice. Here are a few of the top cuts best suited for barbecue.

- **Chops**. Simple pork chops are an underrated choice for home grilling. At the time of this writing, I've become very enamored with pork chops. Lately, we've been purchasing bone-in, heritage breed, mid to thick-cut pork loin chops. These slabs of pork are very easy to prepare and the price cannot be beat. Add the extra boost in flavor you'll get with the bone in and you've got a great grilled meal at a great price.
- **Ribs**. One of the most popular meats in barbecue is pork ribs. It's surprising how many variations there are on this one part of the pig. You have the Saint Louis cut ribs, spare ribs, baby back ribs, country-style ribs, and even rib tips. (I think it's demeaning to call them riblets). Just remember they're all fair game on the grill, and they all require a long, low and slow smoke to get them tender. Baby backs are popular and they come from the top of the rib cage, nearest the spine of the pig. Spare ribs are from the lower portion of the ribs, nearest the belly. The Saint Louis cut is simply a trimmed-up version of the larger spare ribs. It's simply tidying up the spares into that familiar long rectangular shape. When you trim a slab of spare ribs up "St Louis style" you'll end up with a serving

of, you guessed it, rib tips left over. Last, country-style ribs have no bones and are not really ribs but rather part of the shoulder meat.

- **Shoulders or Butts.** The difference in a shoulder versus a butt is distinct in human anatomy, but not as much on a pig. Counterintuitive to its name, the Butt is actually a portion of the top of pig's forelegs or "shoulders." The picnic shoulder is the smaller, lower portion of the shoulder. A whole shoulder makes for spectacular barbecue. But it can be too big for a lot of patio grills and smokers. Plus, it can be an all-day (and night) affair, so it's not as common in the backyard.

- **Hams.** Hams come from the rear of the pig. It's the real butt here. Hams are almost always found in the grocery store already cured and smoked. It's still great on the grill as you really just need to warm it up, but it's even better with added smoke, and can be served hot or chilled. Spiral cuts allow the ham to absorb added smoke and seasoning and make serving a breeze.

- **Pork Loin.** If you don't cook with pork tenderloin, you're missing out. This lean cut is great for both hot and fast grilling or low and slow adventures. The smaller pork tenderloin is very common in grocery stores and is the perfect size for a small family cookout. The larger pork loin cut has a bit more fat and is equally delicious. If you like it on the "pink side", this is a good choice. There used to be a fear of trichinosis with rare pork roasts. However, a few years ago, the USDA reevaluated and loosened its safety recommendations on this. These days it is considered safe to serve pork on the "pink or "rare" side, if you wish.

- **Bacon.** I love bacon, but if I'm being honest, I don't love *grilling* bacon. It's prone to flare-ups and hard to nail the desired texture when you're combining it with quicker cooking foods. Some of the comment trolls on YouTube don't like it, but I often recommend using precooked bacon in appetizers like jalapeño poppers. It will cut your prep time, and it just helps foods cook more easily.

- **Sausage, Franks, and Charcuterie...Oh my!** Sausage can be any combination on meats, but pork is a go-to favorite. You can cure it for charcuterie and prosciutto or combine it with other meats. One trick to boost the fat and flavor quotient of leaner game meat is to grind it together with some fatty pork (shoulder). It makes for a more succulent sausage.

Sure, there are a few more cuts to choose from on a pig, like the shank and the jowl, even feet. But I'll leave those to another day. I like *PIG* cuts and I cannot lie...

Techniques and Trends

I would love to think that pork chops and ribs are an All-American barbecue invention. The fact is, pig farming has been around a lot longer than the USA. Mankind domesticated pigs from wild boars in East Asia thousands of years ago. Through time, we've ended up with the selection of various traits seen in different breeds today. The history books say Christopher Columbus brought pigs with him in his 1493 journey to Cuba, and explorer Hernando Desoto gets the credit for importing thirteen pigs with him when he landed in Florida, making him the real founding father of pork in the Americas.

These days the vast majority of US pork comes from only a few processing plants, which is something that caused a bit of a problem during the recent Covid-19 crisis of 2020. Typically, you'll find mainly Yorkshire hogs in your big grocery stores. However, over the years, the typical US pig has gotten bigger and leaner. So much so, that in the 1980s, the National Pork Producers Council came up with the slogan "The Other White Meat." The branding stuck. And with more targeted breeding, today's swine is bigger, leaner, and perhaps less flavorful than ever.

Specialty Breeds

Although we've all seen and heard of different breeds of pigs, most people don't really think they have a choice in the matter. Fear not, there is actually a growing trend in pork production that champions different breeds for different needs. This trend is an offshoot of the farm-to-table movement that promotes growing and buying local. Some prefer heritage breeds as an alternative to mass pork production. But I like it for another reason: *Flavor.* Better meat for better barbecue is a "trick" I've mentioned elsewhere in this book. This is where you can really work your meat magic. Here are a few of the heritage, or specialty breeds, of pork available, and the reasons they are beloved.

Berkshire
Berkshire hogs are an old English breed probably the most well known. These intelligent pigs are darker in color. They are sought after for better flavor and juiciness. Especially in high-end hams. Other than the Yorkshire pig, the Berkshire is the breed that is most easily found in stores. And there are further grades and families. For example, only special Berkshire hogs are given the level of distinction, "Kurobuta", which carries a premium status similar to "Kobe" in the beef world.

Duroc
Duroc hogs are also noted for great juiciness with a mild flavor. They make for a premium pork chop.

Hampshire Pork
Hampshire is a breed that is sought after in the charcuterie world. It has a very lean meat that is great for salami and gourmet cured meats.

Iberico

Iberico Pork comes from a unique black Iberian pig that comes from the southern parts of Portugal and Spain. It is known for the flavor that comes from the pigs' special diet of acorns and natural vegetation, which gives the meat a nutty flavor.

Mangalitsa

The Mangalitsa is very fatty and used for its gourmet-level lard in dishes like pâtés.

Tamworth

The Tamworth breed has been deemed the World's Best Bacon pig.

Yorkshire

Yorkshire hogs are what most people in the United States will picture and purchase when it comes to pork. It has been bred to abundance and is usually the default choice in stores. It's delicious and lean, but I've come to consider it the baseline in flavor compared to its counterparts.

These special breeds can be found on the menus of fancy restaurants, but they haven't made it to too many butcher counters. I think it's worth the hunt. I keep an updated list of resources on my website, BarbecueTricks.com. A few of the biggest online sources include Porter Road, Meat N' Bone (check out their Iberico specials), Snake River Farms (with beautiful Kurobuta hams) and ButcherBox (Duroc and Berkshire flavorful pork chops). You can also talk to vendors at your local farmers' markets. It's fun to learn from the locals and also support their livelihoods. You'll surely pay more for these special breeds, but you'll be rewarded at the grill. There is an unexplainable depth to the pork flavor they bring to the grill.

Tricks for Perfect Pork

- **Hold it in.** Keep your injection where you want it by using this simple trick. Inject your meat while it's still in the store packaging. You can minimize mess and keep injected marinades from flowing out of your roast by injecting them with marinade and then refrigerating them while they are still in the grocery packaging.

- **Better browning.** If you want to get a better browning or caramelization on your pork chops, be sure they're not too wet. Pat dry your pork chops with a paper towel before cooking. It's hard to brown a pork chop if you try to sear it wet.

- **Picky thermometer.** It's difficult to get a dependable reading in the small space close to the bones of ribs. Instead, use a simple toothpick to measure rib doneness. If the pick slides easily into the meat between the bones, with very little resistance, you're ready to eat.

- **Grinding sausage?** Save time by cutting your meat into one-inch strips instead of cubes. It's less prep and more efficient for many meat grinders.

- **Back to the grind.** You can make your pork easier to handle and grind by giving it an extra chill. Work with slightly frozen (not solid) meat for easier handling and better grinding.

- **Get more white meat in your pulled pork.** Here's how: Smoke one fatty shoulder butt and supplement with a whole pork loin or a big "green" (uncured) ham. You'll end up with a much lighter and leaner mix of meat. The legendary, *Sconyer's Barbecue* in Augusta, Georgia, uses whole hams for their pulled pork barbecue, and you can really taste the difference.

- **The trick to perfect pulled pork.** It's simple, but the trick to tender pull-apart pork is to get it to temperature. You'll want to keep smoking slowly until the internal temperature of the pork hits 205°F. The meat should become soft to the touch (almost jiggly) and easy to pull apart. If there is a shoulder bone, it should slide out easily.

- **Time's up rescue.** If you run out of time to smoke before serving, and your butt hasn't quite hit your target, all is not lost. Although long cooked to at least 165°F, or higher in the center, it's fine to eat. You can rescue your dinner by pulling as much as you can into threads and then shred and mince further with a sharp knife or cleaver. It's not ideal, but I bet your guests will still enjoy it.

- **No more fuel fix.** If you're short on wood or charcoal, you can cut the smoking time on your grill. If you've gotten at least two hours of smoke into your roast, wrap it with foil and finish it off in the oven. You may feel like you've failed, but don't fret; the meat typically absorbs most all the smoke flavor it will during in the first few hours.

- **Curly 'que?** You can keep thinner pork chops from curling up on the grill by scoring the edge of the chop with one or two small ¼-inch cuts through the fatty rim of the chop.

- **Put a ring on it.** There are ways to ensure you get the perfect smoke ring every time. You can help to develop a darker smoke ring by utilizing just a bit of Tenderquick curing salt in your rub. It's a cheat, but it works. Tricks aside, just start low and slow at 225°F, and the smoke should do the rest. The ring also likes to be wet. A spritz or two of juice or vinegar during the first 90 minutes or so of the cook can aid in achieving a smoke ring.

- **Roll your own.** Bacon will keep for a long time in the freezer without sacrificing flavor, but if you only use a few strips at a time, try this storage trick. Separate thawed bacon into strips and roll each slice into a coil. Place the coils on a baking sheet lined with parchment paper and freeze solid. Then place frozen coils into an air-tight container in the freezer and only take out what you need when ready to use.

- **Spoiler alert.** You can keep meats from spoiling by storing them smartly in the freezer. Avoid freezer burn and frost by wrapping the meat twice with plastic wrap, waxed paper, or foil. Then, put it all in a freezer bag with as much of the air squeezed out as possible. Vacuum sealers are great, too.

- **Frozen 2**. One trick to eliminate all the air from Ziplock bags is to submerge the meat-filled bag in water just below the opening to push out the air. Additionally, it can save space to flatten everything out to a single layer. A flat Ziplock bag of ground meat stores (and thaws) much easier.

- **Chilled meat is easier to trim.** Before you prep your meat, pop it in the freezer for thirty minutes or so for better handling.

- **Add a pig's nest.** Burgers are better with bacon. Okay, *anything* is better with bacon. Instead of adding the usual bacon slices that can slide off in a single bite, try building a bacon nest. Julienne your raw bacon into tiny, thin strips. You can then twist them around the end of a fork (like spaghetti) to make a nest, and grill it under a brick to crisp up and flatten.

- **Going whole hog.** Try your hand at a whole hog at least once in your life. Just be prepared. Be ready with a plan to buy, thaw, and store the pig until you're ready to cook.

- **Did I mention bacon?** I praised precooked bacon earlier in this chapter. If you want to make an easy batch of fresh precooked bacon in advance, simply bake it in the oven at 400°F for 15 minutes, cool and store in an air-tight container in the refrigerator until ready to use, or eat as a snack. Be sure to save the drippings for the secret ingredient to **Baked Ranch Potatoes** *(found in Sides Notes)*.

- **Get a grip.** You'll want to remove the tough membrane that lines the inside of the pork ribcage. The trick to making it easier to grasp is a simple paper towel. Loosen up one end with a butter knife. Then, using the dry paper towel for grip, slowly peel off the membrane. You should be able to get it off much easier than with your bare slippery fingers.

Grillustration: Peeling the Membrane

PORK RECIPES

The Baddest Boston Butt
Hickory-Smoked Picnic Pork Shoulder
Mango Country Spare Ribs
Lowcountry Pork Chops
Glazed Applewood Smoked Ham
3-2-1 Barbecued Ribs
Pickled-Pepper Pork Tenderloin
Grilled Butterscotch Bacon
Easy Brats
Whole Hog Done Right
Grilled Margherita Pizza with Italian Sausage
Perfect Pork Roast

Pork Appetizers

Amaze Balls
Piggy Mac
Jalapeno Popper Cheese Grits with Bacon

The Baddest Boston Butt

🍖 10-12 🕐 9-10 hours 🔥 Smoke 🪵 Pecan

The Boston Butt has different names, but it's simply the upper shoulder of the pig. The specific name comes from prior to the American Revolution when butchers in Boston would ship their pork in barrels that were called "butts," common on ships in the Boston Harbor. The trick with pulled pork is that you must keep smoking low and slow until the internal temperature of the meat reaches 205°F. That's when the collagen and fat between the meat fibers melts and becomes succulent enough to pull apart.

1 (8-9-pound) Boston Butt
¼ cup mustard
1/3 cup **Memphis Dry Rub** *(found in Rubs & Pastes)*
1½ cups **Slap Yo Mama BBQ Sauce** *(found in Top This)*, divided
1 cup orange juice
1 cup apple juice
1 cup apple cider vinegar
½ cup salt

1. Rub the Boston butt all over with the mustard and apply the Memphis Dry Rub liberally.
2. Place the butt in a dish or pan and cover with plastic wrap. Refrigerate overnight.
3. Preheat the smoker to 225°F and add wood.
4. Remove the butt from the refrigerator, but do not rinse.
5. In a medium bowl, whisk together ½ cup Slap Yo Mama BBQ Sauce, orange juice, apple juice, apple cider vinegar, and salt. Reserve the remaining BBQ sauce for serving.
6. Pour the juice mixture into a clean spray bottle, reserving 1 cup in the bowl.
7. Using the reserved liquid, fill a meat injector and inject the butt on the top and sides, but not the bottom.
8. Place the butt on the smoker and smoke for 6 hours, spraying with the juice mixture every 2 hours. Minimize peeking. If you're looking it ain't cooking.
9. Spray the butt one more time, wrap it tightly in butcher paper or aluminum foil, and return it to the smoker for about 3-4 more hours. For optimum pulling/shredding ability, do not remove it from the smoker until a digital thermometer reaches 205°F.

10. Unwrap the meat, spray with the remainder of the juice mixture, and let it rest for 15-20 minutes before shredding it with forks or bear claws.
11. Serve the pulled pork with the reserved Slap Yo Mama BBQ Sauce.

 I love to pair my pulled pork sandwiches with a crunchy Coleslaw. Try it with **Sweet Slaw** *(found in **Side Notes**)*.

Hickory-Smoked Picnic Pork Shoulder

🐷 10-12   🕐 9-10 hours   🔥 Smoke   🪵 Hickory

Barbecue doesn't need to be complicated or difficult. In **The Baddest Boston Butt** (previous recipe), you rub, inject, smoke, spray, wrap, smoke again, and spray. This pork shoulder (butt) recipe is even easier, without injecting or wrapping, but don't be fooled by its simplicity—the flavor is amazing.

¼ cup **Canadian Blackened Steak Rub** *(found in **Rubs & Pastes**)*
¼ cup demerara sugar
3 tablespoons smoked paprika
1 (8-9-pound) pork shoulder
¼ cup mustard
Buns, for serving
1 cup **Hot Vinegar BBQ Sauce** *(found in **Top This**)*, for serving

1. In a medium bowl, mix together the Canadian Blackened Steak Rub, sugar, and paprika to form a rub.
2. Coat the meat with the mustard and apply the rub generously all over.
3. Put the meat on a plate, cover it loosely with plastic wrap, and refrigerate it overnight.
4. Preheat the smoker to 250°F and add wood.
5. Remove the pork from the refrigerator but do not rinse.
6. Place the pork shoulder directly on the smoker rack. Smoke for 9-10 hours, resisting the urge to peek more than once or twice to check the internal temperature.
7. Remove the pork shoulder from the heat when the internal temperature on a digital thermometer registers 205°F, and let the meat rest for 15-20 minutes.
8. Place the meat in a large pan and shred it with bear claws or two forks.
9. Serve the pulled pork on buns with the Hot Vinegar BBQ Sauce.

 I recommend buying pork shoulder with the blade bone-in, if you can find it. You'll get better flavor and the bone will act as nature's pop-up thermometer, pulling out with ease when the meat achieves pull-apart tenderness.

Mango Country Spareribs

🐷 4-6   🕐 6 hours   🔥 Smoke   🪵 Cherry

Fruity sweetness is a good match for succulent spareribs. In the US, we often pair pork with apple, but did you know that mangos are the most popular fruit in the world? In fact, they're a symbol of love in India, and delivering a basket of mangos is considered a sign of friendship. I say, if they *really* want to be nice, they can drop off a basket of these spareribs.

2 racks pork spareribs
3 tablespoons mustard
1 tablespoon salt
2 teaspoons freshly ground black pepper
1 cup mango juice
¼ cup Worcestershire sauce
2 tablespoons Thai sweet red chili sauce
1 tablespoon firmly packed brown sugar
3 cloves garlic, finely minced
1 teaspoon onion powder
1 teaspoon ground ginger
1 teaspoon crushed red pepper flakes

1. Preheat the smoker to 250°F and add wood.
2. Remove the membrane on the back of each rack of ribs. Loosen the tough silver skin on one end using a butter knife. Get a good grip on the membrane using a paper towel, peel it off, and discard.
3. Coat the ribs with the mustard and sprinkle with the salt and pepper.
4. Place the ribs directly on the smoker rack and smoke for 3 hours.
5. In a medium bowl, whisk together the mango juice, Worcestershire sauce, sweet red chili sauce, brown sugar, garlic, onion powder, ground ginger, and red pepper flakes.
6. Remove the ribs from the smoker and wrap each rack separately in heavy-duty aluminum foil. Before sealing tightly, baste both racks generously with the prepared mango sauce.
7. Return the ribs to the smoker and continue smoking for 2 hours.
8. Unwrap the ribs and discard the foil.

9. Baste each rack with the prepared sauce again. Return the unwrapped ribs to the smoker rack.
10. Smoke the ribs for 1 hour.
11. Remove the ribs from the heat when the internal temperature on a digital thermometer registers 190°F.
12. Baste the ribs with the sauce once more and let the meat rest for about 5 minutes before serving.

 Sometimes the space between bones is too tight to get a good read from a digital meat thermometer. When your ribs are done and ready to eat, you should see the bones protruding at the ends. Use a toothpick to probe between the bones. If you can insert it into the meat with little resistance, the ribs are ready.

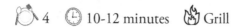

Lowcountry Pork Chops

🍖 4   🕐 10-12 minutes   🔥 Grill

Every time I cook with pork chops, I ask myself why I don't do it more often. They are affordable, quick to prep, and grill fast. If you want to go "next level," try to find chops from a Berkshire hog. If you've only had supermarket pork for years, you'll be surprised by the superior flavor.

4 bone-in pork chops
1 tablespoon mayonnaise
¼ cup + 1 tablespoon **Caribbean Rub** *(found in **Rubs & Pastes**)*, divided
¼ cup (½ stick) unsalted butter

1. Preheat the grill to medium-high heat (350°F-400°F).
2. Generously apply the mayonnaise and ¼ cup Caribbean Rub all over the pork chops.
3. Grill the pork chops for about 5-6 minutes per side, based on desired doneness, but do not remove the meat from the heat until a digital thermometer reaches a minimum of 145°F for safe consumption.
4. Let the pork chops rest for 5 minutes.
5. In a small microwave safe bowl, melt the butter and stir in the remaining Caribbean Rub.
6. Drizzle hot seasoned butter over pork chops to serve.

Pork chops can pair nicely with a wide array of sides. Try these along side the visually spectacular **Braised Cabbage Head** *(found in **Side Notes**)*.

Glazed Applewood Smoked Ham

🕐 10-12   ⏱ 5 hours   🔥 Smoke   📚 Apple

The holiday ham is a feast for the eyes. Add smoke and it's a feast for the nose and mouth, too. The great thing about most ham we usually buy is that it's already cured and smoked by the processor (Once-Smoked). It's considered thoroughly cooked, so all you are really doing is adding your own layer of flavor and warming it up to serve (Twice-Smoked).

1 (10 pound) bone-in, fully cooked, spiral-cut ham
¼ cup **Savory Mustard Sauce** (*found in* **Top This**)
¼ cup firmly packed light brown sugar
1 teaspoon ground cinnamon
1 teaspoon ground cloves
½ cup **Chipotle Honey Glaze** (*found in* **Top This**)
2 apples cut in wedges, for serving

1. Preheat the smoker to 275°F and add wood.
2. In a small bowl, whisk together the Savory Mustard Sauce, brown sugar, cinnamon, and cloves.
3. Place the ham in a disposable aluminum pan and generously apple the mustard mixture all over the ham.
4. Place the pan with the ham in the smoker and smoke for 4 hours, without opening the lid.
5. Add the apple wedges to the pan, and baste the ham and apples with ¼ cup Chipotle Honey Glaze, reserving the remaining glaze for later.
6. Continue smoking for 1 additional hour.
7. Remove the pan from the heat and pour the remaining glaze over the top of the ham and apples.
8. Tent it loosely with aluminum foil and let it rest for 15-20 minutes, before plating the ham and apples to serve.

 Spiral cut hams work great for this recipe. They're easy to serve and the extra nooks and crannies help to soak up additional smoke and glaze.

3-2-1 Barbecued Ribs

🍖 8-10   🕐 6 hours   🔥 Smoke   📚 Cherry

I didn't invent the 3-2-1 method for ribs but I love it, primarily because it's easy to remember. It may be a surprise to you that most competition pitmasters think "fall off the bone" is over cooked. I disagree, but feel free to tweak the times a bit to suit your desired doneness. The final hour of cook time in this technique will allow you to tighten up the bark and help hold everything together with a glaze of sticky sauce.

4 slabs baby back ribs, full racks
1/3 cup mustard
1½ cups **Memphis Dry Rub** (*found in* **Rubs & Pastes**), divided
½ cup apple cider vinegar
½ cup orange juice
1½ cups **Slap Yo Mama BBQ Sauce** (*found in* **Top This**), divided

1. Preheat the smoker to 225°F and add wood.
2. Loosen the thin skin on the back of a rack of ribs and grasp with a table knife and a paper towel. Pull hard to remove, and repeat for each slab of ribs.
3. Generously coat the ribs in the mustard and apply 1 cup Memphis Dry Rub all over the slabs.
4. Pour the vinegar, juice and ½ cup of Slap Yo Mama BBQ Sauce into a clean spray bottle. Set aside.
5. Place the ribs in the smoker and smoke for 3 hours, without peeking.
6. Place each rack on a separate piece of butcher paper or aluminum foil. Sprinkle remaining Memphis Dry Rub all over each and spray generously with the juice mixture before sealing each rack tightly.
7. Put the individually wrapped slabs back in the smoker and continue smoking for 2 more hours.
8. Unwrap the ribs completely, spray with the juice mixture, and then baste with ½ cup Slap Yo Mama BBQ Sauce. Any remaining BBQ sauce is for serving. Discard any left-over juice mixture.

9. Smoke for 1 more hour until the sauce is hot and sticky.
10. For optimal "fall off the bone" texture, remove the ribs from the heat when the meat shrinks away from the ends of the bones, and the internal temperature is 190°F, or above.
11. Let the ribs rest for 5-10 minutes before serving with the remaining Slap Yo Mama BBQ Sauce.

 Rib Tip tip. Trim up the full slab of spares into a St Louis style, as described earlier in this chapter. Be sure to smoke the scraps and enjoy them as a snack that will also help you test your cooking progress.

Pickled-Pepper Pork Tenderloin

🍖 6-8   🕐 16 minutes   🔥 Grill

I first did this recipe with pickled jalapeno juice. I love the heat, but that can leave guests asking for a glass of milk! Here it's tamed by a sweet hot pickle combination.

2 cups **Fridge Pickles & Peppers** (*found in Nuts, Cheese, Desserts & More*), divided
¼ cup soy sauce
¼ cup red wine
2 tablespoons olive oil
2 (1½-pound) pork tenderloins
1 teaspoon garlic powder
1 teaspoon onion powder
1 teaspoon freshly ground black pepper
¼ cup chopped green onions

1. In a small bowl, whisk together ½ cup of the pickle juice, soy sauce, red wine, and olive oil.
2. Place the tenderloins in a dish and pour the marinade over, turning to coat all sides.
3. Refrigerate the pork for 4 hours and discard the marinade, but do not rinse the meat.
4. Preheat the grill to medium-high heat (350°F-400°F).
5. In a small bowl, combine garlic, onion, and pepper.
6. Sprinkle the rub on the tenderloins and place on the grill.
7. Grill 8 minutes per side and remove from the heat when a digital thermometer reaches 145°F.
8. Let the meat rest for 10 minutes.
9. Slice the pork tenderloins and top with the remaining Fridge Pickles & Peppers to serve.

 Boost the flavor of every bite by asking your butcher for a Heritage breed of pork. Berkshire is a great choice for tenderloin.

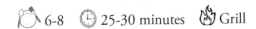

Grilled Butterscotch Bacon

🍖 6-8   🕐 25-30 minutes   🔥 Grill

Candied bacon like this Butterscotch Bacon is a cardiologist's nightmare. But it's a barbecue lover's dream. The salt, sweet and savory pork combine to create a new food group that somehow is better than you can even imagine. Chances are your guests haven't tried it before, so it's a fantastic conversation starter.

1 pound (12 slices) thick-cut bacon
1 cup brown sugar
½ cup (1 stick) butter, melted
1 tablespoon crushed red pepper flakes

1. Preheat the grill to 325°F.
2. Using metal skewers, thread a piece of bacon loosely on each skewer, stretching out the slice.
3. In a small bowl, whisk together brown sugar, butter and pepper flakes, until the sugar has dissolved.
4. Place the skewers in a dish and pour the marinade over, turning each piece to coat the bacon well. Reserve the marinade for basting.
5. Place the individual skewers on the grill and cook for 15 minutes, turning twice.
6. Baste the bacon skewers with the marinade and smoke for 10 more minutes, turning and basting once more during this time.
7. Remove the skewers when crisp and bubbly.

Match your store-bought bacon with the wood you may be adding to your grill. Applewood and hickory smoked bacon are common choices at the market. Thick cut will hold up better on a skewer but it's not imperative. Go with your personal preference.

Easy Brats

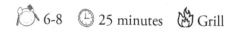 6-8   🕐 25 minutes   🔥 Grill

Brats are a great tailgate food. Just remember that, unlike hot dogs, they are uncooked raw meat. You'll need to cook them to an internal temperate of 160°F, but don't fret. The long bath in simmering liquid that you use here will allow you plenty of time to easily get them fully cooked while keeping them deliciously moist.

2 pounds uncooked brats (8 links)
2 (12-ounce) cans beer or chicken stock
8 hot dog buns, for serving
Savory Mustard Sauce *(found in **Top This**)*, for serving
Fridge Pickles & Peppers *(found in **Nuts, Cheese, Desserts & More**)*, for serving

1. Preheat grill to medium-high heat (350°F-400°F).
2. Place a cast iron skillet on the grill and pour in the beer or chicken stock.
3. Add the brats. They do not have to be covered by the liquid.
4. Close the grill lid and cook for 20 minutes, turning once or twice.
5. Remove the brats from the beer bath and place them on the grill grate.
6. Discard the liquid and sear the brats for 5 minutes, turning often to sear all sides.
7. Remove the brats from the heat when a digital thermometer registers 160°F, and place immediately in buns.
8. Serve with Savory Mustard Sauce and Fridge Pickles & Peppers.

 Brats can be made out of beef, veal or pork. The ones most common here in the US are labeled all premium pork on the packaging. However, bratwurst is an old German name. It is derived from brät, which translates to finely chopped meat, and wurst, which means sausage.

Whole Hog Done Right

🌀 80-100　🕐 12-13 hours　🔥 Smoke　🪵 Hickory

Whole Hog is a lot of work. But it's worth it. It's a specialty that's high in the BBQ hierarchy but also falls in the unusual category of being uncommon. Whole hog competitions are a dying breed, and truthfully there is a lot of waste in cooking a whole hog versus butts. In the backyard, a whole hog is just usually too big, and only a few brave restaurateurs are up for creating the infrastructure needed. If you just want pulled pork for a crowd, smoke several Boston butts, but if you want an experience, go whole hog.

3 cups **Memphis Dry Rub** (*found in **Rubs & Pastes**)
2 cups **Canadian Blackened Steak Seasoning** (*found in **Rubs & Pastes**)
2 cups kosher salt, divided
2 cups firmly packed light brown sugar, divided
3 cups apple cider vinegar, divided
3 cups apple juice, divided
1 whole (80-100-pound) hog, head removed, split and spine cut
1 (28-ounce) bottle mustard
Trio of Sauces, for serving (*all found in **Top This**):
Hot Vinegar BBQ Sauce, **Southern BBQ White Sauce**, and **Slap Yo Mama BBQ Sauce**

1. In a large container, mix together Memphis Dry Rub, Canadian Blacked Steak Seasoning, 1 cup salt and 1cup brown sugar, to make the rub.
2. In a separate container, combine 2 cups apple cider vinegar, 2 cups apple juice, the remaining salt and the remaining brown sugar. Stir until all dissolved and set aside to be used for the injection sauce.
3. Pour the remaining apple cider vinegar and the remaining apple juice into a clean spray bottle to be used as a mop sauce during smoking.
4. The butcher should have removed the head, split the pig and cut the spine. Lay the pig on a large flat surface, such as a raised table, covered with butcher paper for easier handling and clean-up.
5. Trim out any organs remaining, and pull the spinal cord out from the sides and discard.
6. Pull off the membrane from the ribs and check to see if there are any visible areas of sinew or silver skin that need to be cut away.
7. Use a hose to thoroughly clean the hog inside and out.

8. Preheat the smoker to 250°F and add wood.
9. Pour the entire bottle of mustard on the hog and spread over all sides until well-coated.
10. Apply the rub all over by really packing it on and pressing it into the meat.
11. Using a meat injector, fill the syringe with the injection sauce and inject the shoulders, hams and loins, until full.
12. With help, place the seasoned and injected hog directly on the smoker, skin-side down.
13. Smoke for about 12-13 hours, spraying with the mop sauce every 2 hours. There is no need to turn the hog, if placed on skin-side down originally.
14. The hog is done when a digital thermometer placed in the hams reaches 185°F-195°F, and when placed in the shoulders, reaches 196°F.
15. Carefully, and with help from at least 3 other people all wearing heat-resistant gloves, remove the entire grate holding the hog and gently carry it to the serving table.
16. Remove any pooled grease and discard. Leave the hog on the grate for serving, or slide the hog off the grate onto a table covered in butcher paper.
17. Separate and cut the ribs for ease in handling, and serve the hog "pig-pickin' style" with the trio of sauces.

 Should you have your butcher include the head and hoofs? It's totally up to you. You'll likely pay for it either way unless you're charged by the pound, so use Grill real estate, presentation, and what you are personally willing to deal with in clean-up, as the guide.

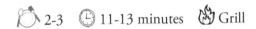

Grilled Margherita Pizza with Italian Sausage

🍳 2-3   🕐 11-13 minutes   🔥 Grill

Pizza on the grill is a lot of fun, but it can also be one of the most challenging dishes to get right. Be sure to start with a firm dough and use a pizza peel to transport the dough on and off the grate smoothly. Practice makes perfect.

½ teaspoon onion powder
½ teaspoon oregano
½ teaspoon salt
½ teaspoon freshly ground black pepper
1 (½-pound) Italian sausage link
1 bakery pizza dough
1 tablespoon olive oil
¼ cup **Garlic Quattro Formaggi Topping** (*found in* **Top This**), heated through
2 tomatoes, sliced
6-7 fresh basil leaves, torn
4 ounces fresh buffalo mozzarella cheese, thin sliced and cut in quarters

1. Preheat the grill to medium heat (300°F-350°F).
2. Combine onion powder, oregano, salt, and pepper. Set aside.
3. Place the sausage link on the grill grate and grill for 4-5 minutes per side until browned.
4. Slice the sausage and set aside.
5. Spray a baking sheet with cooking spray and roll out the pizza dough onto the pan, shaping round or rectangular, about ¼" thick.
6. Brush the top of the crust with olive oil and carefully slide the crust onto the grill grate.
7. Grill for 2-3 minutes until it starts to brown slightly.
8. Gently turn the crust over and reduce the grill temperature to low (250°F-300°F).
9. Top the pizza with the warmed Garlic Quattro Formaggi Topping, then add sliced Italian sausage, sliced tomatoes, and torn fresh basil leaves.

10. Sprinkle the seasoned salt mixture over all, and scatter the mozzarella pieces on top.
11. Grill the pizza with the lid closed for about 5 minutes until the crust is browned and the cheese is hot and bubbly.

 Using a real Pizza Peel makes handling your dough much easier. I recommend using a layer of coarse corn meal to help the dough slide on and off the peel more easily, and it does not affect the flavor.

Perfect Pork Roast

🕑 8   🕐 56-66 minutes   🔥 Grill

Pork loin is a delight to cook on the grill. It's quick cooking and packs a lot of juicy flavor. It's also affordable. Look for a larger and fattier pork loin roast instead of the more common (and smaller) tenderloin.

2 tablespoons **Homemade Chili Powder** (*found in Rubs & Pastes*)
2 tablespoons firmly packed light brown sugar
2 tablespoon kosher salt
2 teaspoons garlic powder
2 teaspoons onion powder
2 teaspoons freshly ground black pepper
1 (3-4-pound) pork loin roast, boneless
½ cup **Smoky Sweet Plum Sauce** (*found in Top This*), divided
3 teaspoons chopped green onions, for serving

1. In a small bowl, whisk together the Homemade Chili Powder, brown sugar, salt, garlic powder, onion powder, and pepper to make the rub. Set aside.
2. Trim the roast as needed and tie with kitchen string to hold its shape.
3. Season the entire roast with the rub and place the meat in a dish. Cover with plastic wrap and refrigerate overnight.
4. Preheat the grill to medium-high heat (350°F-400°F).
5. Place the pork on the grill and cook for 16 minutes, turning once, to sear.
6. Reduce heat to medium-low (300°F-325°F).
7. Continue grilling the roast for 35-45 minutes, until a digital thermometer reaches 145°F.
8. Brush the pork roast with half the Smoky Sweet Plum Sauce and raise the grill temperature to medium-high again.
9. Grill for 5 minutes with the lid closed until the sauce is hot and sticky.
10. Remove the pork from the heat and let it rest for 10 minutes.
11. Sprinkle the meat with green onions and serve it with the remaining sauce.

 You'll sometimes find these long loins sliced into loin chops. If you're ready to splurge, ask your butcher for a heritage breed like Berkshire, and you'll get splurge-worthy flavor.

PORK APPETIZERS

Amaze Balls

Makes 20-24 balls   25 minutes   Grill

Amazing. That's a great way to describe the flavor blast you get in one bite of these Italian inspired cheese-stuffed meatballs. The trick is to work with the baby mozzarella cheese curd balls that are readily available in grocery stores.

2 pounds ground sausage
½ cup finely grated parmesan cheese
½ cup breadcrumbs
1 egg, beaten
1 tablespoon Worcestershire sauce
1 teaspoon garlic powder
1 teaspoon onion powder
1 teaspoon dried oregano
1 teaspoon dried basil
1 teaspoon salt
1 teaspoon freshly ground black pepper
1 teaspoon crushed red pepper flakes
¼-½ cup chicken broth, as needed for liquid
1 pound fresh baby mozzarella cheese balls

1. In a large bowl, using your hands, mix together uncooked ground sausage, parmesan cheese, breadcrumbs, egg, Worcestershire sauce, garlic powder, onion powder, oregano, basil, salt, pepper, and red pepper flakes, until well-combined. Add enough chicken broth to make the mixture stick together, but do not add too much.
2. Starting with one baby mozzarella cheese ball, form 2 tablespoons of the sausage mixture all around and shape into a golf ball-sized meatball, completely enclosing the cheese. Repeat the process until there are about 20-24 Italian meatballs stuffed with cheese.
3. Preheat the grill to medium-high heat (350°F-400°F).

4. Place the prepared meatballs on the grill and cook for 25 minutes, turning once or twice.
5. Remove the meatballs from the heat when a digital thermometer in the meat reaches 165°F, and let the meatballs rest for 5-10 minutes before serving.

 When you are working with raw meat you always want to make sure you hit the recommended internal temperature of 160°F for all ground meats. The recommendations were updated a few years ago to 145°F for "whole" meats and 165°F for all poultry. Because these meatballs are stuffed with cheese in the middle, you'll have no problem hitting your target.

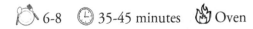

Piggy Mac

🍽 6-8   🕐 35-45 minutes   🔥 Oven

What to do with leftover BBQ? This is an excellent side dish to serve with ribs, or it can stand alone as a meal in itself!

1 small red onion, coarsely chopped
1 jalapeno, seeded and finely chopped
4 cups sharp cheddar cheese, shredded & divided
2 cups heavy whipping cream
8 oz cream cheese, softened
2 tablespoons all-purpose flour
1 teaspoon salt
1 teaspoon pepper
16 oz elbow macaroni, cooked according to package directions
2 cups **Hickory-Smoked Picnic Pork Shoulder** *(found in this chapter)*
½ cup **Slap Yo Mama BBQ Sauce** *(found in **Top This**)*
½ cup Panko breadcrumbs

1. Preheat oven to 375°F.
2. In a large bowl, stir together onion, jalapeno, 2 cups cheddar cheese, heavy whipping cream, cream cheese, flour, salt, and pepper until well-combined.
3. Stir in the hot cooked pasta, pulled pork, and BBQ sauce.
4. Pour the mixture into a 13x9x2 oven-proof baking dish.
5. Top with the remaining cheese and sprinkle with the Panko breadcrumbs.
6. Bake uncovered in the preheated oven for 35-45 minutes, until hot and bubbly.
7. Serve immediately as a side or as the main dish.

 Serve this meaty mac as a main dish and pair it with the **Crispy Brussels Sprouts** *(found in **Side Notes**)*.

🥩 8-10   🕐 1 hour+15-30 minutes   🔥 Smoke   🪵 Apple

The main reason you don't see grits in many barbecue books is because they tend to fall through the grates of the grill! Ha! Avoid that mess. Instead, we solve that problem with a grill pan to keep it together. You'll find that grits do a great job of absorbing delicious applewood smoke flavor.

1 cup quick-cooking grits (not instant) cooked in chicken stock instead of water
2 tablespoons minced garlic
2 teaspoons salt
2 teaspoons freshly ground black pepper
2 jalapenos, chopped
1 small onion, chopped
1 cup sour cream
½ cup cream cheese, softened
½ cup Half 'n Half
2 eggs, beaten & tempered
8 slices **Grilled Butterscotch Bacon** (found in this chapter), cooked and coarsely chopped
1 cup cheddar cheese, shredded
1 cup parmesan cheese, shredded
1 sleeve Ritz crackers, crushed
4 tablespoons (½ stick) butter, melted

1. Preheat the smoker to 275°F and add wood.
2. In a large bowl, stir together cooked grits, garlic, salt, pepper, chopped jalapenos, chopped onions, sour cream, cream cheese, Half 'n Half, and tempered beaten eggs, until well-combined.
3. Fold in chopped bacon, cheddar cheese, and parmesan cheese.
4. Spray a disposable aluminum foil pan with cooking spray, and pour the grits into the pan.
5. Place the pan in the smoker and smoke for 1 hour.
6. Spread the Ritz cracker crumbs over the grits, and drizzle the melted butter over the crackers.

7. Continue smoking for 15-30 minutes until browned and bubbly.

8. Let stand for 5 minutes before serving to firm up.

 This recipe can be baked in the oven to speed things up. Preheat oven to 350°F. Prepare the ingredients as directed above and pour into a 9"x13" casserole dish. Bake for 40-45 minutes until browned and bubbly. Let stand for 5 minutes before serving to firm up.

Talking Chop: Greg Rempe from The Barbecue Central Show

Greg Rempe is the creator and host of The Barbecue Central show. It's longest running barbecue show in existence. It's radio, it's a podcast, and it's on video too. Catch him every week as he chats with competition and pro pit masters. He was kind enough to chat with me about everything from grills to meat. Here's a slice of our discussion; edited for time and clarity.

BW:

You have a ton of grills! What do you grill with when you're just in the backyard?

GR:

I've really started to thin out because I've become a fan of my Traeger Timberline 850 that Traeger gave me a couple of years ago. That thing is just incredible. It works really well. It accommodates a lot of meat. Pellets are very easy. So I like that one. I love my Green Mountain grills. I have two of those in different sizes. I actually have a prime line of theirs. It's in the garage that I just haven't put together yet. So that's three.

I have a Lang 36 inch offset stick burner that I love when I have the time. But I got to have the time in order to use that. And if I have the time the stick burner provides the single best tasting barbecue that you can get! Certainly my opinion. But I can sit here and line up pitmaster after pitmaster that says a stick burner provides the best barbecue if that's what you're able to cook on.

I've given away a bunch of stuff that I don't use or I've gotten something new when I only have a limited amount of space on the patio. But those are the ones that I'm using now. I think I'm right in the neighborhood at six or seven right now.

BW:

Which one would you definitely not get rid of?

GR:

I want to keep all of them right?! That's why I have them. I think if I had to give all of them up except the one out of the current setup that I have, I would keep the Green Mountain grill, a "Jim Bowie."

BW:

What is that? Is that a pellet grill?

GR:

Yeah, that's a pellet cooker. It's got good space. It's not inefficient if you are only doing a small cook. It does accommodate that pizza oven insert that you can get. So you can do a completely different cooking style with it. *If I had a Weber kettle, I would probably say that!* I don't have a Weber right now.

BW:

So do you have a soft spot in your heart Weber kettles? Specifically their Smokey Mountain model?

GR:

Oh yes. It's easily the most recommended beginner barbecue pit. If you're just looking to add something that's pretty quick to learn it doesn't require a lot of time... like the stick burner does. Weber Smokey Mountain is something that I love. I had a pair of them at one point and you just get to learn that thing! It is set it and forget it once you have that whole thing figured out. I mean, I absolutely love those.

BW:

And guys are winning contests on those!

GR:

Yes. This is the original. Yeah.

BW:

What do you like to cook?

GR:

I would be lying if I said that I love to cook brisket. My results have been a mixed bag at best and that's shameful for me to say. What do I cook really well? Pork butt. But I think anybody can really produce a great pork. I mean they're so forgiving. I really like them cause they yield a lot of meat and if you don't eat through that in the first setting, you have a number of different ways that you can go with leftovers.

I love barbecued ribs. My favorite ribs are done on the Lang. Again, we go back to the whole flavor and a smoke profile. That thing moves so much air that I can do a rack of ribs that would take me five hours on the Traeger or the Green Mountain grill, in three hours on the Lang because the amount of air flow. I mean, right around the same temperature! Because it is just moving so much air it gets done much quicker.

I think you gotta be careful with ribs. People go to "three, two, one method" and I'm here to tell you that is a bunch of bull and you can end up with a overly cooked rib! Remember that "two" part is two hours in the foil! It's going to steam. I call it the super heating method. So if you're not careful or you don't have an extremely meaty rack of ribs, you're going to be able to go in and pick that bone up and the meat is going to stay right there kinda like meat mush! So, depending on what texture, you like... I'm not going to sit here and judge it too much, but I like a little bit more texture. I don't like it to pull off the bone; but, instead, bite. There's *a little tug* and it pulls away, clean from the bone. *That's* really what I'm going for.

BW:
Well, if you were to adjust the "three two one" method, what would the numbers be?

GR:
You know, depending on the temperature that you're cooking. I like to go 275°F to 300°F. I would go two to three hours outside of the smoke. One hour max in the foil. Then back out to tighten up a half an hour, to 45 minutes, maybe.

BW:
Any other key secret ingredients that you go to.

GR:
I like to do avocado oil on the top. Avocado is a neutral oil. It's got a higher smoke point, it has nothing to do with flavor. It just solely a rub adherence. Some people love the mustard thing. When I got into it, 14 years ago, there was this rub called the Texas barbecue rub. A guy by the name of Bill Cannon did it. He had a pretty popular forum back in the day as well. His method was to shake worcestershire sauce on the brisket, or the pork butt or the ribs, and rub that in. And then apply the rub on top of that. So you actually ended up with a paste, if you will. So I'll still do that from time to time. But the oil seems to be where I'm going to the most. It's easy and you know there's

no flavor profile at all on it. And do the rub, let it sit in. Yeah. I mean that's pretty much it. No other secrets. I'm not injecting.

BW: What's your typical smoking wood?

GR:
Up here? We get a plethora of Cherry. It's more expensive than, you know, Hickory and some of the other stuff. But I like my choices cherry. If I have a decent amount of Hickory and I'm using the stick burner, I will burn that with a ribs or pork butts just because I think Hickory and pork work really well together.

BW:
I know you talk to the pellet producers. Have you tried charcoal pellets?

GR:
Look, here's another thing that we want to make sure that we're telling folks... If somebody is passing off a charcoal pellet, it is 100% complete B.S.! They're selling you a bill of goods. It's not true. My friends at Cookinpellets.com do NOT make a charcoal pellet. I have had this discussion with Chris Becker, the owner of Cookinpellets.com about that. They just don't. It would be a terrible product. (Note: Becker says it's complicated to explain, but simply it would be hard to make it right). tThere's wood in there or they're just lying to you. It's one of the biggest scams going right now. Almost as bad as when the propane re-fillers didn't tell anyone that they were taking your 20 pound bottle and were only allowed to fill it back up (exchange) to 15 pounds. So if you have bottles, take them to a propane refill station, where they will refill to 20 pounds.
BW:
I didn't know that! Sounded legit to me! Do you have a favorite barbecue joint?

GR:
Favorite barbecue restaurants across the country? Well, as you know, I traveled nowhere. So, in Cleveland I would say there's only three currently that I'm recommending. Mabel's BBQ downtown. That's a Michael Symon owned restaurants, right on East Fourth street. Killer barbecue. It's really good. If you're going because you like sauces, you're going to be wildly disappointed because he only has one sauce on the table. It's a mustard based sauce and more regionally it's a Bertman's ballpark mustard based sauce, which anybody outside of Cleveland has no idea what the hell that is. But it's kind of an offshoot of a Dijon feel. But it's gray. Like this mustard is gray for real. So if you've ever seen it outside of basically Ohio...

If you know about it, you are from Cleveland and that's it. Otherwise you don't know anything about, and it's a good sauce, but that's it. There's a hotter sauce that they can bring out from the back called Aardvark sauce. They don't have 50 sauces like a lot of these other places.

Then on the West side of Cleveland, there's a place called Proper Pig. I know the owners there, they do it right. And then on the near West side, about a mile from where my office is, there's this place called Barbecue Smokehouse. It's the best in Cleveland as far as I'm concerned. He's got a Southern Pride smoker out in the back.

BW:
Let me fire off some rapid fire questions and you can give the first thing that pops into your head. What is your favorite cheese?

GR:
American. Regular, old American.

BW:
How do you like your steak?

GR:
Medium rare.

BW:
Got a favorite chef?

GR:
Michael Symon.

BW:
What do you like on your hot dog?

GR:
Ketchup

BW:
Is a single hotdog a meal or a snack?

GR:
That's a meal.

BW:
Wagyu. Is it worth it?

GR:
Yes.

BW:
What's your specialty?

GR: Talking.

CHAPTER 8

FISH & SEAFOOD

"If wishes were fishes, we'd all have a fry."
—Anonymous

Sometimes it seems like the only seafood people like to grill is Salmon. It is definitely the favorite fish to smoke in North America. Its oily flesh is perfect for absorbing smoke flavor. It's also nice and firm, and holds up to well to rough handling. However, plenty of other water dwellers also take on smoke nicely. I'm on the coast of South Carolina, where local shrimp and oysters are favorites from the sea.

If you want to exercise your smoker with seafood, just remember the fattier the fish, the more the smoky flavor will be absorbed. Salmon and trout have high-fat content and are excellent on a smoker. You'll need a dependable grill that can reliably sustain the lower smoking temperatures that allow fish to slowly absorb the subtle flavors without overcooking the delicate meat.

Just like with smoked meats, the process of smoking fish started as a way of not only cooking, but also preserving the food. The bold flavors and superior health benefits have continued to stand the test of time.

It used to be that fishing and serving the bounty of the sea were limited to specific seasons, but with the modern fishing industry, lots of different kinds of seafood is readily available any time of year. Plus, flash-freezing techniques help it all taste better. Smoked shrimp and lobster are luxurious smoking experiments you can easily tackle in any season. I say eat what you want when you want it.

When shopping for fish to grill or smoke, start close to home. Think local. Here in Charleston, we go through a lot of South Carolina local shrimp. In the Pacific North, salmon is the go-to. You can get your hands on everything these days, so definitely cook what you like, but sourcing close to home means keeping things fresh!

Fish Picking

Freshness is always important when shopping for seafood. If you're examining whole fish, keep your eyes on the eyes. The eyes of the fish should look clear and bright with fresh-looking gills and an overall shine. With fillets, it gets a bit trickier. They may have been previously frozen and that's not always bad. Just know that regulations say that fact must be disclosed on the label. It could very well be better than a never-frozen fillet that's been lingering too long. Last, it's fair to judge the cleanliness of the store, where the smell should be like the sea; fresh and clean like the ocean. If you smell ammonia, then you'll want to shop somewhere else.

With salmon, decide if you're going to go with farm-raised Atlantic salmon or the pricier, wild-caught, variety. The flavor is better in the wild-caught fish, but make sure it looks and smells just as fresh. Another factor, it's typically only available in the spring and summer months.

Fishy Future

One recent development in the centuries old world of seafood is genetically engineered fish. Just a few years ago a US firm was approved to sell genetically engineered salmon in Canada. The company says its quick-growing fish can grow to full size in just 18 months. Critics question the seafood's safety and also have ecological concerns. The verdict is still out on the flavor.

I don't know - last night I enjoyed a delightful smoked leg of salmon and I feel fine – Ha!

Stupid Fish Tricks

Cooking fish and seafood over a live wood fire has been a technique long before we came up with the word barbecue. Here are a few easy tricks to get the best out of your seafood:

- **Shop for fresh fish by examining with your nose first.** Fresh fish should smell clean and briny, not "off" or overly fishy. The eyes should appear shiny and full, not cloudy or sunken. Skin and scales should look shiny and metallic. With fillets, the flesh should be firm and bright (not dull) and never slimy.
- **Smoking fish with the skin.** Leaving the skin on can help the meat retain its moisture, but you don't want to eat all kinds of fish skin. Many people love the taste of salmon skin when fried crisp. But smoking will not crisp the skin to many people's liking. Simply leave it on one side of the fish to help you move it around on the grill.
- **Ease the clean.** Grill mats and screens can help with both clean up and maneuverability of delicate fish on the barbecue. If you don't own them, just remember that many upright smokers, especially electric smokers, have grill grates that are easily removed for cleaning and loading/unloading food. Give yourself easier access by removing the grates you don't need. Plus, use this feature to load and remove food where there is more room.
- **Above the surface.** To get the most out of fish on the smoker, you should choose thin-skinned fish for the best absorption of smoke flavors. Avoid using foil that will block exposure to smoke. If you're fast grilling, pat the fish dry completely before you place it on the oiled grill. The dry surface will help promote browning instead of steaming.
- **Keep shrimp fresh longer.** You can purchase shrimp with the head on or off. I say go head off. The preparation is obviously easier, and because the head contains a lot of the shrimp's tiny organs, it spoils faster. Headless shrimp are less perishable and will keep longer.
- **Choose a side.** I hate it when I try to flip over a kebab of shrimp to have them spin on the skewer and defeat my attempt to grill the other side. Double skewer smaller pieces, in parallel on each end. Two skewers make flipping easier.
- **Quick thaw.** It's best to slowly thaw your fish filets overnight, covered, in the refrigerator set below 38°. However, in a pinch, you can also "quick thaw" by placing the vacuum-packed fish in cold water and letting it defrost. Refresh with room temperature water often to hasten the process.
- **Skin side down.** Place the fish skin-side down on the grate. It will act as a protective layer for the more delicate meat. And you can grill delicate fish atop a bed of thin-sliced lemon to add protection from sticking, as well as flavor.
- **Non-stick tricks.** It's no secret that fish sticks to the grill. The trick to minimize the sticking is to fully oil the grate. First, preheat the grate. Then, use tongs and a cloth or paper

towel dipped in vegetable oil to paint oil on the grill grates to prevent sticking later. In addition, resist moving the meat until you are fully ready to flip.

- **Bowling for pin bones.** One trick to finding pin bones in raw fish is to examine each piece over the bottom of a mixing bowl. Drape longer fish filets over an inverted bowl. Then, the bend in the surface of the flesh will allow you to feel and easier locate the tiny bones with your fingers. Remove them with sanitized needle-nose pliers.

- **Trick to getting fishy smell off your hands.** Sure, you could wear rubber gloves, but here is a way to stop it before it starts. Simply wash your hands with plain cold water before you handle the fish. It will minimize odors after.

- **Best oil.** One of the best oils for grilling fish is peanut oil. It's gotten a bad rap lately because of the rise in allergies, but peanut oil helps bring out the flavor of fish and not overpower it. Plus, it's always a good choice on a grill because of its higher scorch point and ability to handle high heat.

- **Freezer tip.** You can better preserve fish for later grilling by freezing seafood fully submerged in water first. Then, after thawing, you can use the fishy liquid leftover to feed your plants.

- **Get even.** Fish fillets that taper will cook unevenly on the grill. Tricky chefs will fold the thinner tailpiece up and over to create a more uniform thickness and even cook time.

- **Flipping awesome.** A fish spatula is one accessory that is a must if you cook a lot of seafood. This special tool is a slotted, thin, and flexible spatula that is the perfect tool for lifting and moving delicate foods. Always slide the spatula under the fish in a motion parallel to the grill grate to minimize sticking and flaking.

- **Flip tip.** Sometimes you need to go wide. If you don't own an extra-wide fish spatula, try using *both* of your hands, carefully removing longer grilled fillets with *two* regular kitchen spatulas. Remember to always slide them under the meat moving parallel to the grate for the cleanest result.

SEAFOOD RECIPES

Cedar Plank Shrimp
Mango Fish Tacos
Seared Tuna Steaks
Grilled Fish Fillets
Hot Grilled Oysters
Grilled Soft-Shell Crab
Sugar-Crusted Savory Salmon
Cajun Crab Legs
Shark Week Steaks
Grilled Lobster in Lemon Butter
Garlic Grilled Scallops
Salt-Crusted Grilled Whole Red Snapper

Seafood Appetizers

Crab-Stuffed Mushroom Caps
Salt Block Shrimp & Pepper Skewers
Hot Crab & Artichoke Dip

Cedar Plank Shrimp

2-3   6 minutes   Grill

There are a bunch of good reasons to try your hand at plank grilling. The fragrance of both the wood and the smoke infuses your seafood with intense flavors. The plank acts as a nice trick to buffer the seafood from burning over high heat. Last but not least, it looks so darn cool. It's like nature's unprocessed, paper plate. You can eat right off the plank.

Cedar planks for grilling
¼ cup (½ stick) butter, melted
3 tablespoons **Seafood Spice Rub** (*found in* **Rubs & Pastes**)
1 pound large shrimp, peeled & deveined
1 tablespoon olive oil
2 tablespoons lemon juice, for serving
2 tablespoons chopped fresh parsley, for serving

1. Soak the cedar planks in water for 2 hours.
2. Preheat the grill to medium-high heat (350°F-400°F).
3. In a medium bowl, whisk together butter and Seafood Spice Rub, until blended.
4. Reserve half the seasoned butter for basting later.
5. Toss the shrimp in the remaining seasoned butter.
6. Remove the cedar planks from the water, pat dry and oil just the top of each with olive oil.
7. Place the planks directly on the grill grate and arrange the shrimp on the planks in a single layer.
8. Grill the shrimp for 3 minutes per side, basting halfway through with the remaining seasoned butter.
9. Sprinkle lemon juice over the shrimp and top with the chopped fresh parsley to serve.

Shrimp are sold by the "count" number. It's a calculation of the number of shrimp per pound. If you see a "U" attached to the number that means "under" or less than. Typically, Jumbo shrimp are 21/25. Small shrimp are U/50 and the large shrimp we use are generally 31/35.

Mango Fish Tacos

 4   🕐 10 minutes   🥣 Kitchen

Fish has a bad reputation for sticking to the grill. With this dish it's not a problem. If they do stick, the solution here is to make fish tacos. You're breaking it down into chunks anyway.

Grilled Fish Fillets *(found in this chapter)*, grilled
1 mango, diced
1 bell pepper, diced
½ cup chopped green onions
8 corn tortillas, for serving
1 cup **Sweet Slaw** *(found in **Side Notes**)*, for serving
1/3 cup **Jalapeno Salsa** *(found in **Top This**)*, for serving

1. Gently flake the cooked fish and place in a medium bowl with the chopped mango, diced green pepper, and chopped green onions.
2. Toss lightly to combine.
3. Fill each corn tortilla with the mango fish mixture, 2 tablespoons Sweet Slaw and 1-2 teaspoons Jalapeno Salsa.

 Keep the south of the border vibe flowing by enjoying a light Pilsner-style lager.

Seared Tuna Steaks

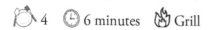 4   🕐 6 minutes   🔥 Grill

Tuna is the world's most popular fish. But there is more to tuna than tuna salad sandwiches. In fact there are over fifteen different varieties of tuna to explore across the sea. The most common varieties are albacore, bluefin, skipjack and yellowfin. Tuna is not only tasty, but it's packed with healthy omega-3s, so tuna is definitely good for your heart.

1 teaspoon kosher salt
1 teaspoon freshly ground black pepper
4 (6-ounce) tuna steaks
1 tablespoon olive oil
4 cloves garlic, minced
Grilled Garlic Bread Bruschetta *(found in **Nuts, Cheese, Desserts & More**)*, for serving

1. Preheat the grill to medium-high heat (350°F-400°F).
2. In a small bowl, stir together salt and pepper and set aside.
3. Rub the tuna steaks with the olive oil and the garlic.
4. Sprinkle with the salt and pepper mixture.
5. Place the tuna on the directly on the grate and grill for 3 minutes per side for medium, or to desired doneness, but do not remove from the heat until a digital thermometer reaches 140°F, for safe consumption.
6. Slice the steaks and serve with Grilled Garlic Bread Bruschetta.

 Add a heaping helping of the **Skillet Cornbread Salad** *(found in **Side Notes**)* and your guests are sure to walk away satisfied.

Grilled Fish Fillets

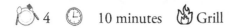 4   🕐 10 minutes   🔥 Grill

When you are grilling fish you'll want to start with a fillet that's firm enough to hold up to the grill and light enough to absorb some smoke flavor. Popular white fish for grilling include tilapia, Mahi Mahi, cod, catfish and snapper. Flatfish in the flounder family work well, too. Why grill flatfish? Oh, just for the halibut.

1 teaspoon garlic powder
1 teaspoon smoked paprika
1 teaspoon dried thyme
1 teaspoon freshly ground black pepper
½ teaspoon kosher salt
2 tablespoons olive oil
4 (6-ounce) cod fillets (or halibut or tilapia), thawed

1. Preheat the grill to medium heat (300°F-350°F).
2. In a small bowl, combine garlic powder, paprika, thyme, pepper, and salt until blended.
3. Rub the fish fillets with olive oil and coat with the prepared seasonings.
4. Oil the grill grate, or a nonstick grill mat, or perforated pizza screen.
5. Place the fish on the grate and grill for 5 minutes per side.
6. Remove the fish when a digital thermometer registers 145°F.

 Keep delicate filets from sticking to the grill by generously lubricating the grill grate with oil and refraining from flipping too soon.

Hot Grilled Oysters

🧺 Makes 1 dozen   🕐 15 minutes   🔥 Grill

Here in Charleston, oyster roasts are a lot of fun. The only downside is that it's a lot of work to shuck each bite. Plus, these "roasts" don't really include any real roasting. The oysters are all typically steamed by the sackful. Well, I'm here to put the *roast* back into the oyster roast! These beauties are both roasted over smokey fire and, then, served on the half shell.

½ cup (1 stick) butter, melted
¼ cup Parmesan cheese, grated
2 cloves garlic, minced
3 tablespoons chopped fresh parsley, divided
2 tablespoons Worcestershire sauce
2 tablespoons hot sauce
1 teaspoon cayenne pepper
1 dozen raw oysters

1. Preheat the grill to medium heat (300°F-350°F).
2. Whisk together melted butter, Parmesan cheese, garlic, 2 tablespoons parsley, Worcestershire, hot sauce, and cayenne pepper.
3. Sprinkle coarse sea salt in the bottom of a cast iron skillet, and place the oysters on top, using the salt to stabilize them.
4. Top each oyster with a tablespoon of the butter mixture.
5. Grill the oysters for about 15 minutes, until hot and bubbly.
6. Remove the oysters from the grill and top with the remaining parsley to serve.

 Grilled oysters are best in the winter months. You can remember the specific months by talking like a pirate. Remember matey, the months always end with "RRRRrrrrrr."

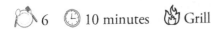

Grilled Soft-Shell Crab

🦀 6   🕐 10 minutes   🔥 Grill

My first experience with soft-shell crab was at the now defunct Remy's restaurant on Hilton Head Island. I was freaked out by the idea of eating the crazy crustacean on a bun, but that was deep fried and in a sandwich, so it didn't take much prodding to get me to try it. I'll eat anything deep fried. With soft-shell crab you're eating the shell and all. It's intimidating, but dazzling on the grill.

¼ cup **Citrus Chile Butter Paste** *(found in **Rubs & Pastes**)*, melted
12 soft-shell crabs, cleaned and gills and apron removed
Kicked-Up Dipping Sauce *(found in **Top This**)*, for serving

1. Preheat the grill to medium heat (300°F-350°F).
2. Generously brush the crabs all over with Citrus Chile Butter Paste, and place on the grill rack.
3. Grill the crabs for 5 minutes, turn them over and baste with more butter.
4. Grill for 5 more minutes and remove the crabs from the heat.
5. Let the crabs cool slightly and serve warm with the Kicked-Up Dipping Sauce.

 Contrary to what people think, the soft-shell crab is not a distinct breed of crab. It's typically a simple blue crab that has recently molted its hard shell as a normal part of the growth cycle.

Sugar-Crusted Savory Salmon

🐟 10-12   🕐 1¼-1½ hours   🔥 Smoke   🪵 Maple

Smoked salmon is a dish that has drawn a lot of people into the world of smoking meat. It's interesting to differentiate the different varieties - grilled salmon, cured and cold smoked salmon, and even lox. Lox are not smoked at all – just salt brined.

Here we "hot" smoke the salmon at 200°F.

1 quart cold water
½ cup salt
3 cups firmly packed light brown sugar, divided
1 (3-5-pound) salmon
½ cup (1 stick) unsalted butter, melted
1 tablespoon freshly ground black pepper
4 chicken bouillon cubes, crushed
1 lemon, cut in half for serving
¼ cup chopped fresh chives, for serving
4 ounces cream cheese, for serving

1. In a large container, stir together water, salt and 2 cups of brown sugar to make a brine.
2. Stir until dissolved and submerge the salmon in the water.
3. Cover and refrigerate 4 hours.
4. Remove the fish from the brine, but leave it in the refrigerator, uncovered, for 3 more hours.
5. Whisk together the melted butter and the remaining brown sugar.
6. Add the wood to the smoker, but do not preheat.
7. Oil the smoker rack, or a nonstick grill mat, or perforated pizza screen.
8. Remove the salmon from the refrigerator and season all over with the black pepper and crushed bouillon cubes.
9. Place the fish skin-side down in the cold smoker, turn the heat to 200°F, and smoke for 30 minutes.
10. Baste the salmon with half of the sweetened butter.

11. Continue smoking for 45 minutes – 1 hour until the meat flakes easily with a fork, and a digital thermometer reaches 145°F.
12. Remove the salmon from the smoker, and baste with the remaining sweetened butter.
13. Plate, sprinkle with lemon juice and chopped fresh chives, and serve with cream cheese.

For a hot & fast variation on the grill, try soaking 2 cedar planks in water for an hour and cutting the salmon into two filets. Place the salmon filets on the planks, skin-side down. Sprinkle 2 tablespoons of **Seafood Spice Rub** *(found in **Rubs & Pastes**)* over the filets. Place the cedar planks with prepared salmon on a grill preheated to medium-high heat (350°F-400°F), and grill for 25 minutes, until a digital thermometer reaches 145°F and the flesh flakes easily with a fork.

Cajun Crab Legs

 4   30 minutes   Smoke   Oak

My first judgement of a new barbecue joint happens the moment I step out of my car in the parking lot. Do I smell smoke? If so, it's a good sign. If not, they aren't smoking on site. With any great barbecue meal, the flavor starts with your nose first, then your eyes, and finally, your taste buds. Crab legs never smelled or tasted this good.

½ cup cocktail sauce
2 tablespoons hot sauce (optional)
2 teaspoons prepared horseradish (optional)
½ cup (1 stick) butter, melted
1 tablespoon Cajun Seasoning
4 snow crab leg clusters
1 lemon, cut into wedges, for serving

1. If you like your cocktail sauce hot, whisk together the cocktail sauce, hot sauce, and horseradish in a small bowl. If you prefer a milder taste, leave out the hot sauce and horseradish and set the cocktail sauce aside for serving.
2. In a separate small bowl, whisk together the butter and Cajun seasoning. Divide the Cajun butter in half.
3. Preheat the smoker to 250°F and add wood. Oil the grill grate, or a nonstick grill mat, or perforated pizza screen.
4. Place the crab legs on the smoker rack and smoke them for 20 minutes.
5. Baste the crab legs with half of the Cajun butter and smoke them for 10 minutes.
6. Remove the crab legs from the heat. The meat should be opaque and firm.
7. Serve the crab legs with the remaining Cajun butter, prepared cocktail sauce, and lemon wedges.

 Be sure you have some shellfish crackers to break into the crab legs. I mean the tool, not saltines. Kitchen shears can also be a great assist.

Shark Week Steaks

 4   50 minutes – 1 hour   🔥 Smoke   🪵 Alder

Shark needs to be handled carefully and given a refrigerated buttermilk bath right after it's caught and cleaned, or it will likely be almost inedible. Shark can taste really gamey, and it also spoils easily. A milk bath eliminates that funky gamey taste, as well as the ammonia smell of blue shark. Mako sharks don't have the same smell, but they still benefit from the milk bath. Buying from a reputable source will ensure your shark has been properly processed and is safe to consume.

2 pounds shark meat (Mako or blue), cut into 4 steaks
1 cup orange juice
¼ cup olive oil
¼ cup soy sauce
2 tablespoons lemon juice
1 tablespoon Worcestershire sauce
1 tablespoon minced garlic
1 teaspoon freshly ground black pepper
2 tablespoons olive oil
¼ cup **Garlic Pear Seasoning Paste** *(found in **Rubs & Pastes**)*
1 (15-ounce) can pears in syrup, drained and cut into small chunks, for serving

1. Trim any dark meat off the shark steaks, if it hasn't been done already, as it doesn't have a pleasing taste. If the skin is still intact, leave it on to lock in moisture during cooking, because there isn't much fat on shark.
2. Whisk together the orange juice, olive oil, soy sauce, lemon juice, Worcestershire, garlic, and pepper to make a marinade.
3. Place the shark steaks in a shallow container and pour the marinade over them. Cover the dish and refrigerate it for 1 hour, turning once.
4. Preheat the smoker to 275°F and add wood.
5. Remove the shark steaks from the refrigerator, discarding the marinade, and rinse the steaks.

6. Coat with olive oil and the Garlic Pear Seasoning Paste.
7. Oil the grill grate, or a nonstick grill mat, or perforated pizza screen.
8. Place the steaks on the smoker rack. If the skin is still intact, place them skin-side down.
9. Smoke the steaks for 50 minutes - 1 hour, until a digital thermometer reaches 145°F.
10. Remove the steaks from the heat. If the skin is still intact, remove it before serving (it will not be edible). Serve the steaks hot, topped with chopped pears.

 Flash-freezing techniques are getting better and better every day. Still, fresh shark will always taste much better than frozen.

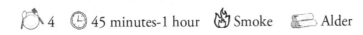

Grilled Lobster in Lemon Butter

🦞 4   🕐 45 minutes-1 hour   🔥 Smoke   🪵 Alder

You have to wonder who first looked at a lobster and though that it might be good as a snack. The truth is our gourmet lobster was considered poor man's food back in Colonial America. It was *that* plentiful. By the 1880s it benefited from becoming a commodity as one of the first ever canned foods. From there, prices went up as railroad dining cars glorified the dish even further. Today fresh lobster is still readily available, but much more expensive. It is easy to grill, though. I suggest celebrating the purchase of your next new grill with this Instagram worthy feast.

4 fresh lobster tails
1 cup (2 sticks) butter, melted, divided
Juice of 2 lemons
2 cloves of garlic, minced
2 teaspoons Cajun seasoning
1 teaspoon kosher salt
½ teaspoon freshly ground black pepper

1. Preheat the smoker to 225°F and add wood.
2. Grasp the lobster shell and split the top of each tail with heavy duty kitchen shears, cutting down front to the last tail segment. Gently pull out the front end meat and rest it on the split shell with the base of the tail still attached. Rinse well inside the shell.
3. Split the center of the meat to spread out slightly.
4. In a medium bowl, stir together melted butter, lemon juice, garlic, Cajun seasoning, salt, and pepper. Reserve all but 2 tablespoons for serving.
5. Drizzle each tail with 1 tablespoon of the prepared butter.
6. Place the tails in the smoker with the split-side up, and smoke for 45 minutes – 1 hour, basting once with 1 tablespoon of the prepared butter.
7. The lobster is done when a digital thermometer reaches 130°F-140°F. They should be opaque and firm to the touch.
8. Serve the lobster with the reserved butter mixture.

Keep it fancy, yet delicious and serve with the **Corn Pudding** (*found in* **Side Notes**).

Garlic Grilled Scallops

🕐 4-6   🕐 4-6 minutes   🔥 Grill

Scallops hold a soft spot in my heart as they were a favorite of my late father. They're an impressive and fancy dish to prepare on a hot grill. But beware. A recent investigation found scallops to be the seafood leader for having the most impostors. The study found almost half of the scallops sold in stores were actually skate or stingray trimmed in cookie cutter like pieces. You can spot the fakes by looking at the thickness, firmness and texture. A fake will be more dense with fewer distinct fibers and may also taper like a skate. The real deal won't be perfectly uniform and cylindrical, so be mindful.

3 tablespoons olive oil
Juice of 1 lemon
6 cloves garlic, minced
2 teaspoons kosher salt
2 teaspoons freshly ground black pepper
1 teaspoon onion powder
2 tablespoons chopped fresh dill
1 pound fresh scallops
½ cup **Remoulade Burger Topping** *(found in Top This)*, for serving

1. In a large bowl, whisk together olive oil, lemon juice, garlic, salt, pepper, onion powder, and dill.
2. Toss the scallops in the marinade and let stand for 10-15 minutes.
3. Preheat the grill to medium-high heat (350F-400°F).
4. Oil the grill grate, or a nonstick grill mat, or perforated pizza screen, and arrange the scallops in a single layer.
5. Grill 2-3 minutes per side until lightly charred.
6. Remove the scallops from the heat and serve immediately with Remoulade Burger Topping.

 Make quick work of peeling fresh garlic cloves by giving the paper wrapped cloves an overnight soak in water. The skin will peel off easily by hand the next day.

Salt-Crusted Grilled Whole Red Snapper

🕐 4   ⏱ 25-30 minutes   🔥 Grill

Salt crusted snapper is another dish that makes the average pitmaster appear to be a gourmet mad scientist. It's a wild looking mountain of salt!

Don't worry. You won't be ingesting all that sodium. Most of the salt will break away and leave you with a deliciously seasoned bite.

2 (1½-2-pound) whole red snappers, scaled & gutted
4 pounds kosher salt
1½-2 cups water, as needed
1 lemon, sliced
6 cloves garlic
2 tablespoons chopped green onions
2 tablespoons chopped fresh cilantro

1. Rinse the fish, and using a paring knife cut small, shallow slits about an inch across the top of each fish to score.
2. Preheat the grill to medium-high heat (350°F-400°F).
3. Add the salt to a large bowl, and slowly stir in the water, as needed, to make a slushy type salt mixture.
4. Cover 2 perforated pizza screens with aluminum foil.
5. Mound a quarter of the salt on each foil pan and spread out to the length of the fish.
6. Top the mound of salt on each pan with a snapper.
7. Stuff each fish cavity with half the lemon slices, half the garlic cloves, and half the chopped green onions.
8. Cover the fish with the remaining salt "cement" mixture, top to bottom.
9. Place the screens on the grill grate and grill for 25-30 minutes.

10. Remove the fish from the heat when a digital thermometer reaches 145°F, and crack and cut away the salt crust immediately. If left on too long before the cook, or after, the fish will be too salty.
11. To serve, plate the fish, sprinkle with the chopped fresh cilantro, and pull out the lemon slices from the cavity to place on top of the fish.

 Did you know that Salt was one of the world's first currencies? In fact, Roman soldiers were once paid in salt. It's actually where the word "salary" comes from.

SEAFOOD APPETIZERS

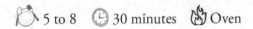

Crab-Stuffed Mushroom Caps

🍳 5 to 8   🕐 30 minutes   🔥 Oven

Vegetarians and dietitians love mushrooms because they are chock full of B and D vitamins, and are anti inflammatory. They also offer a bit of protein. Apologies in advance to the vegetarians because we're stuffing our mushroom caps with crab in this recipe. But feel free to prepare a few without the meat for guests with special dietary requests.

16 ounces cooked crabmeat
2 (8-ounce) blocks cream cheese, softened
8 slices bacon, cooked and crumbled
1 cup shredded Parmesan cheese, divided
1 teaspoon freshly ground black pepper
20 mushrooms, cleaned and stems removed

1. Preheat oven to 375°F.
2. In a medium bowl, mix together cream cheese, bacon, ½ cup Parmesan cheese, and pepper.
3. Stuff the mushrooms with the crab mixture and place them on a baking sheet.
4. Sprinkle remaining Parmesan cheese over the tops of all.
5. Place the baking sheet in the oven and bake for 20-25 minutes until bubbly.
6. Serve warm.

 At your next gathering, pair these mushroom caps with a cold Dark Brown Ale.

Salt Block Shrimp & Pepper Skewers

🍽 4   🕐 36 minutes   🔥 Grill

Pink Himalayan salt blocks are an adventurous way to season, cook and serve grilled foods. Plus, it's a great conversation starter when you are grilling for guests. Just be sure you don't over salt by adding any additional salt mixed in with other seasonings.

2 tablespoons unsalted butter, melted
2 garlic cloves, minced
3 tablespoons honey
Juice of 1 lemon
1 teaspoon freshly ground black pepper
½ teaspoon cayenne pepper
1 pound large shrimp, peeled and deveined
1 small onion, cut in quarters and petals separated
1 bell pepper, cut into 2-inch pieces
1 red pepper, cut into 2-inch pieces
Himalayan Salt Block
Summer Salad (*found in* **Side Notes**), for serving

1. In a medium bowl, whisk together butter, garlic, honey, lemon juice, pepper, and cayenne pepper to make a marinade.
2. Toss the shrimp, onion petals and pepper pieces in the marinade.
3. Thread the marinated shrimp, peppers, and onions onto metal skewers in an alternating fashion. Try to allow the shrimp to make some contact with the salt when later placed on the block. Reserve the marinade for basting while on the grill.
4. Place a completely dry Himalayan salt block on the cold grill grate.
5. Heat the grill to low and then increase the heat gradually, 50° at a time, until 400°F is reached (about 10 minutes).
6. Allow the salt block to cure on the grill for 20 more minutes at 400°F.
7. Place the skewers on the salt block and cook for 3 minutes.

8. Brush with more marinade, turn the skewers over, and continue cooking for 3 more minutes.
9. Serve hot alongside Summer Salad.

 Himalayan salt blocks can crack if they are heated too quickly with direct heat on the grill. Raise the temperature slowly.

Hot Crab & Artichoke Dip

 12   ⏱ 25-35 minutes   🔥 Oven

We took two of the most difficult foods to clean and married them together in a dip that's one of the *easiest* to eat. Thankfully most of us buy our crab and artichoke already prepared for quick cooking. This dip is perfect for either a casual or fancy tailgate.

1 (14-ounce) can artichoke hearts, coarsely chopped
½ pound cooked crabmeat
8 ounces cream cheese, softened
1 cup mayonnaise
1 cup Parmesan cheese
½ cup chopped onions
1 tablespoon minced garlic
1 teaspoon freshly ground black pepper
½ teaspoon cayenne pepper
¼ cup chopped green onions
Butter crackers, for serving

1. Preheat oven to 350°F.
2. In a large mixing bowl, combine artichoke hearts, crabmeat, cream cheese, mayonnaise, Parmesan cheese, onions, garlic, pepper, and cayenne pepper.
3. Spray a pie dish with cooking spray.
4. Pour the crabmeat mixture into the pie dish and bake for 25-35 minutes, until hot and bubbly.
5. Sprinkle chopped green onions over the top and serve hot with crackers.

 For a recipe variation, replace the crabmeat with an 8-ounce bag of fresh spinach leaves and voila, hot spinach artichoke dip!

My YouTube and GrateTV.com co-host, Jack Waiboer, is a former butcher and South Carolina State Barbecue competition champion. Oh, and he's a great friend, too. Jack is the first person I thought about when I decided to include these "Talking Chop" segments into this book. It's been a few years since I talked barbecue with him, but it amazes us how many people are still discovering our old videos.

Jack is a true traditionalist when it comes to barbecue. He's taught me all about charcoal and whole animal barbecue. So I was a bit surprised to hear that he is yet another pitmaster that has become a fan of sous vide barbecue. In fact, *just about every one* of my Talking Chop pit-masters mentioned they are enjoying this new "bag, cook and grill" trend. Similarly, many also mention their affinity for Big Green Eggs.

Here's a transcribed segment of a recent conversation when we caught up on what's cooking with the Carolina Pitmaster and meat prophet. It's lightly edited for clarity.

BW:
What are you cooking at home these days?

JW:
I'm cooking a lot of chicken. We're cooking a lot of vegetables at my house right now. Believe it or not, my wife is eating better these days than she was before. So it's all higher quality. And that includes a lot of vegetables. So we're doing a lot of vegetables at the house. I cook it on the Big Green Egg as much as I can.

BW:
Is the Big Green Egg your "go-to" grill?

JW:
You know, the Big Green Egg sits right there on my patio. So it's the first one out the door. Of course I still have all the other grills and everything that you need to compete with.

I've been messing around a lot lately with sous vide. I've been dropping steaks in a bag of boiling water or *simmering water*, I should say. Then, using different searing techniques. It's a good time.

BW:
What's the last meat you prepared via sous vide?

JW:

I did a 45 day dry aged ribeye and a prime tenderloin for mother's day!

BW:

What's your overall take on sous vide in barbecue?

JW:

I'm enjoying it. It's a nice technique. You know, the cool thing about it is when you do this for a while you understand the different techniques of cooking meat, and how it's all done. I'm not bragging, but I can cook a "perfect steak" pretty much any way I want to cook it. So, whether you do it in the reverse sear or the straight cook, or however you're smoking, or whatever you're doing, sous vide is just another technique to game that.

And what's cool about it is… it's really not all that that hard, Bill. You put the steak in the water and let it go for an hour or two. Then you hit it on a super-hot surface. Sear it on the outside. A Big Green Egg does perfect for that. And you know, I've also used a cast iron frying pan for sear. I've been really messing around with that technique and having a lot of fun and learning something new.

I'm still kind of messing around with sous vide chicken. I'm having a difficult time with it *mentally*. I understand the science of the chicken, but *not* cooking a piece of chicken to 165 degrees. After a career in the restaurant business it's not necessarily something that you can just let go! So it's hard to get over that. I did it, and I felt good about it. I didn't have any health issues or anything with it. It just was different. I was just very apprehensive about that!

BW:

It's time for my rapid fire questions. What's your favorite meat to cook at home?

JW:

A steak.

BW:

How do you like your steak?

JW:

Medium rare

BW:

Is Wagyu worth it?

JW:
Yes.

BW:
What is what's your favorite heritage breed of Pork?

JW:
I'd have to say a Duroc hog.

BW:
What is the best barbecue joint you've ever visited?

JW:
Sweatman's Barbecue (Holly Hill, SC) in the old days.

BW:
Your favorite chef?

JW:
Thomas Keller.

BW:
What do you like on your hotdog?

JW:
Mustard, onions, and chili.

BW:
One hot dog… meal or snack?

JW:
Snack.

BW:
What is your favorite cheese?

JW:
Muenster.

CHAPTER 9

NUTS, CHEESE, DESSERTS AND MORE

"Age doesn't matter...
Unless you are a cheese."
—Billie Burke

Your grilling adventures aren't just limited to meat. When you expand your world to smoking, you can have a lot of fun. Some grills can control temperatures so well you can experiment with baking in them, too.

Nuts

Lately, I've been living in a low carb world. I've become addicted to eating and smoking whole pecans. I'll try to stop long enough to write about a few things other than just nuts.

Most nuts are fair game on the smoker. However, they can burn quickly at higher temperatures over 320°F, if you don't keep an eye on them. Thankfully they are a better match for low and slow temperatures (the same temperatures you use to smoke meat, like 225°F). The more time they spend in the smoke, the more smoke flavor. Try to match the wood to the nut (i.e., pecan wood for pecans) - even better. Unlike cheese, you don't need a cold smoker for nuts.

Ideally, shop for and choose raw nuts (not already roasted). These are easily found in larger grocers, health food stores, and club stores like Sam's and Costco. Costco has great prices on bulk pecans, almonds, and even walnuts.

For the sweetest option, try cashews as we do in this chapter's first recipe. Cashews feature more sweetness and natural sugar than most any other nut. They're mainly grown and imported from Africa and India, but 90 percent of the world's cashews are consumed in the United States.

If your mind isn't blown yet, realize this... a cashew isn't even a nut. It's the seed of a fruit. Mind blown.

Fruit

You may be wondering if fruit has any place on the grill. It is a wonderful option for desserts to enjoy. Typically, fruits are grilled hot and fast rather than slow smoked. Fruits great for grilling include pineapple, plantains, and most firm stone fruits. These fruits can be enhanced by including a bit of char from the sugars caramelizing on the fruit more than the absorption of smoke.

- Great on the grill: I've enjoyed grilling fruit kebabs basted with sweet syrups and rum concoctions.
- Not so much: I tried a smoked watermelon that mimics the look of a beautiful red roast. The flavor was okay; however, the texture of hot or even warm melon is not appealing. A bunch of people have tried to brine and smoke these melons as a savory dish as well. Interesting and telling that few have done it more than once!

If you're looking for an elegant pairing for fruit, smoked or not, fruit pairs nicely with smoked nuts and cheeses.

Cheese

One of the most popular foods to smoke other than meats is cheese. Between all the different varieties of cheeses and the different smoke flavors you can infuse into them, there are literally thousands of combinations.

This is an arena where wood smoke really shines. It's a real joy to be able to take an inexpensive chunk of cheddar and turn it into something really special. Cheese is very easy to smoke, you just need to stick with a firm cheese and the ability to keep it from melting through the grates while it smokes. This is made possible by a technique called cold smoking.

Cold Smoking

Cold smoking is a unique form of smoking that involves maintaining steady smoke at much lower temperatures than most smokers are made to do. Most electric smokers and pellet grills are limited to about 180°F on the low end. For cheese, you need to keep the temperature below 90°F for best results.

If you're looking to smoke cheese or cold-smoke salmon regularly, invest in an add-on accessory that will allow you to truly cold smoke. Some companies like Bradley Smokers have special boxes you can buy to simplify the job. However, if you just want to cold smoke occasionally, you can invest in a small smoker tube. These perforated steel tubes are sized to fit on the grill. They allow you to burn wood chips or pellets for hours without reloading and without producing significant heat.

They're handy, and not just for cold smoking, but also for adding extra smoke to any grill top.

Tricks for Nuts, Fruit and Cheese

Nuts and cheeses always make for great snaking. Make it even better with the perfume of hardwood smoke. Here are a few tricks to make it easy:

- **Let it mellow.** Nuts and especially cheese, can benefit from a rest just like meat. With cheese, one trick is to smoke it and then leave it, wrapped in plastic, in the refrigerator overnight to allow for the smoke flavors to continue to seep into the cheese. It will mellow and taste even better with a bit of time.

- **Spoiler alert.** If you want to extend the life of cheese, you can store it in the refrigerator and prevent mold by placing a paper towel dampened with a bit of white vinegar in the bottom of a sealable plastic container. You can also add a few cubes of sugar to the bottom of the container, so if there is the slightest infiltration of mold, it will feed on the sugar before the cheese.

- **Think small.** When smoking smaller bites like nuts or fruit pieces, you can use a grill mat or tray to suspend the bits from falling through the grate. These screens allow for smoke and air circulation to the bottom of your food and also keeps everything portable to move on and off the smoker. I like using inexpensive perforated pizza pans to do the job.

- **Worth its salt.** Here is the easiest recipe in this book: Smoked Salt. You can simply keep a pie pan filled with coarse kosher or sea salt in the smoker chamber when you do your next brisket or butt. A few hours will infuse the granules with a subtle smoke flavor that can be a secret ingredient on popcorn.

- **Flipping for fruit.** Fruit is another one of those foods that will spin on kebabs when you try to flip them on the grill. Double skewer your fruit with two sticks to help maneuverability.

- **Put the squeeze on lemons.** Your long-handled barbecue tongs can do more than just flip fajita meat. Insert half lemons or limes inside the joint of the tongs, then use the leverage of the tong handles to easily squeeze out more juice than you could with your bare hand. Great for a flourish over a pan of sizzling fajitas.

- **Fruit flavor.** Fruits work best on the grill when you take advantage of their sweetness. Brush fruit pieces with brown sugar, cinnamon or lemon juice to highlight the fruit's inherent flavors.

- **Make cheese grate again.** You can make hard cheeses easier to grate by spraying your grater with a sheen of cooking or butter spray. This will keep the cheese from sticking stubbornly to the grater and make cleanup easier. Same for the blades in your food processor.

- **Sliced and diced.** Soft smoked cheeses like mozzarella can be difficult to slice cleanly with a kitchen knife. One trick is to use dental floss (unflavored, no mint) or a typical hard-boiled egg slicer to breeze through the thinnest slices.

- **Roll your own.** You can turn any regular grill into a cold smoker. Keep the heat off and just add slow smoke from a smoker tube or a smoker pouch with wood chips. Check out the stainless-steel perforated tubes made by A-maze-n Products on the resources page at BarbecueTricks.com.com or roll your own tube or pouch and fill it with wood pellets. Ignite it from the ends and add plenty of holes, to help keep it smoldering slowly.

NUTS, CHEESE, DESSERTS & MORE RECIPES

Cashews with Sea Salt & Chives
Cold-Smoked Cheese
Hot Spot S'mores
Blackberry Cobbler
Seasoned Smoked Pecans
Fridge Pickles & Peppers
Fruit Kebabs with Prosciutto
Breakfast Frittata
Saltine "Potato" Salad
Subway Fatty
Grilled Garlic Bread Bruschetta
Skillet Biscuits
White Banana Pudding
Roasted Pear Crostini
Grit Cakes

Cashews with Sea Salt & Chives

 12 🕐 1 hour 🔥 Smoke Pecan

Smoked cashews are perhaps the biggest smoking trick around. Start with larger "colossal" sized nuts and watch them disappear.

½ cup butter, melted
1 tablespoon Worcestershire sauce
1 tablespoon dried chives
2 teaspoons sea salt
1 teaspoon garlic powder
2 pounds unsalted cashews

1. Preheat the smoker to 250°F and add wood.
2. In a large bowl, whisk together butter, Worcestershire sauce, chives, sea salt, and garlic powder.
3. Add in cashews and toss to coat.
4. Spread the nuts in a single layer or a baking sheet, and place in the smoker.
5. Smoke for 1 hour, and stir every 15-20 minutes.
6. Remove from the smoker and let cool.
7. Store in an air-tight container for 3 weeks.

 Also works well for almonds, pecans, peanuts, and walnuts.

Cold-Smoked Cheese

🔥 Makes 1 pound   🕐 2 hours, Mellowing: 1-7 days   🔥 Smoke   🪵 Apple

Cold smoking can be a small challenge for typical smokers. But don't let that stop you—it's a relatively easy way to take cheese to the next level. Just a hint of smoke turns a cheap chunk of cheddar into an epicurean delight.

To cold smoke, you just need smoke without heat. Aim to keep your cooking chamber below 90°F. This is easier said than done, because most smokers can't maintain low temperatures over time. If you're using a charcoal smoker, ignite just a single chunk of charcoal and stoke with bits of wood through the smoke. Some electric smokers have cold-smoking attachments you can purchase, and often you can simply enlist the help of a smoker tube that generates smoke from wood chips and pellets.

1 pound of hard cheese, such as cheddar, Swiss, or Gouda, room temperature

1. Add applewood to the smoker but do not preheat it.
2. Cut the cheese into 4-inch by 2-inch blocks and blot them dry.
3. Place the cheese blocks on the smoker rack, away from any heat source, but near the smoke "exit" vent.
4. With the smoker cold, light a full smoker tube and place it on the rack to generate a long, slow source of smoke.
5. Continue generating smoke with as little heat as possible. Keep the smoking chamber just under 90°F, for about 2 hours. Place a pan of ice in the cooking chamber to lower the temperature, if necessary. Really keep an eye on this, especially if the smoker is in the sun.
6. Remove the cheese blocks from the heat and blot them dry before wrapping them in wax or parchment paper.

7. Place the smoked cheese blocks in the refrigerator for 1 to 7 days to allow the flavors to mellow. The longer the better.
8. Store the cheese in an airtight container for up to 3 weeks. Slice to serve.

 You don't have to avoid cold smoking completely during the hot summer months, but consider waiting until sundown. You can also chill the smoke chamber by placing two-liter bottles of frozen water inside it. A bowl of ice in the cooking chamber helps, too.

Hot Spot S'mores

Makes 12   8-10 minutes   Smoker   Apple

This recipe does double duty for me. First, it's an easy way to make "just right" s'mores. Secondly, it helps you do a bit of research on your smoker.

By placing these stacked treats at different places in your smoker, you can get a visual read on any possible hot spots you may have, like in the biscuit test in Chapter Two. After 8 minutes of smoking, take a good look at the status of the marshmallow and chocolate. Snap photos so you can remember the results for summers to come. You may be tempted to place foil under the s'mores, for ease of cleanup, but resist if you are trying to get an accurate read on air and temperature flow.

Sugar shouldn't burn below 320°F, but you should see evidence where the cooking chamber gets the hottest. Some of the chocolate and marshmallows may start to melt more quickly than others, or even brown/toast early.

12 graham crackers, halved
6 milk chocolate bars, halved
12 jumbo marshmallows

1. Following the manufacturer's specific start-up procedure, preheat the smoker to 275°F, and add apple wood.
2. Place 12 graham cracker halves in different spots on the smoker rack.
3. Stack each with ½ chocolate bar and 1 marshmallow.
4. Smoke the s'mores for about 5 minutes for a slightly gooey texture, and 10 minutes for the perfect melty marshmallow.
5. Top the stacks with the remaining graham cracker halves after smoking.

 If you're not trying to use this as an exercise to figure out hot spots, try this variation on this campfire treat: Stuff waffle cones with any combination of chocolate chips, mini marshmallows, sliced berries, butterscotch chips, sliced bananas, and mini peanut butter cups cut in half. Wrap each cone tightly with aluminum foil and place on a grill preheated to medium for 5-10 minutes. Unwrap and serve the melty goodness in a cone.

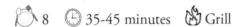

Blackberry Cobbler

🍢 8   🕐 35-45 minutes   🔥 Grill

Desserts on the grill are as flashy as they are delicious. Remember sugar can burn quickly on the grill. Because you're working with higher heat and a lot of sugar for this recipe, you need to work with a thick walled baking pan or, ideally, a Dutch oven. Cast iron works best.

2 cups firmly packed light brown sugar, divided
1 cup (2 sticks) unsalted butter, divided
1 quart blackberries
1 cup all-purpose flour
2 teaspoons ground cinnamon
1 teaspoon baking powder
1 teaspoon salt
1 cup milk or cream
2 eggs, beaten
Vanilla ice cream, for serving

1. Preheat grill to medium-high heat (350°F-400°F).
2. In a 7.5-quart cast iron Dutch oven, add 1 cup brown sugar and 1 stick butter.
3. Stir until the butter is melted and the sugar dissolved; about 4 minutes.
4. Add the blackberries and stir to coat, leaving it on the grill.
5. In a medium bowl, melt the remaining stick of butter in the microwave. Stir in remaining brown sugar, flour, cinnamon, baking powder, salt, milk, and eggs.
6. Stir the blackberries again, and reduce the heat to medium-low (300°F-350°F)
7. Pour the batter evenly over the berries in the Dutch oven and cover with the lid.
8. Cook for 25-30 minutes, until a toothpick or knife inserted in the middle comes out clean.
9. Cool for 10 minutes before serving with ice cream.

 This works equally well with peaches, blueberries, strawberries, or raspberries, instead.

Seasoned Smoked Pecans

🍳 6   🕐 1 hour   🔥 Smoke   ▭ Pecan

Pecans are my favorite nut to smoke. The roasting not only gives the nuts an additional layer of flavor from the smoke, but also gives the mix a satisfying crunch. Keto dieters, like me, love pecans because they tout a lower carb load than most nuts. I like to go "next level" protein and keto crunch by adding a handful of pork rind pieces to my smoked nuts to make a snack mix.

1/3 cup butter, melted
1 tablespoon Cajun seasoning
1 tablespoon Worcestershire sauce
1 teaspoon onion powder
1 teaspoon garlic powder
½ teaspoon cayenne pepper, optional
1 pound pecan halves

1. Preheat the smoker to 250°F and add wood.
2. In a medium bowl, whisk together melted butter, Cajun seasoning, Worcestershire sauce, onion powder, garlic powder, and cayenne pepper (if using).
3. Fold in the pecan halves and stir until well-coated.
4. Spread the nuts out on a baking sheet in a single layer.
5. Place the baking sheet on the smoker rack and smoke for 1 hour, stirring occasionally.
6. Remove the pecans from the heat and let them stand to dry for 10 minutes before serving.
7. Place in an air-tight container to store.

 For a sweet variation, try using maple wood and season the melted butter with the following: 1 tablespoon brown sugar, 2 teaspoons vanilla, 1 teaspoon cinnamon, 1 teaspoon all-spice, and 1 teaspoon salt. Smoking time and temperature remains the same. The spice possibilities are endless!

Fridge Pickles & Peppers

 Makes 3 pints   5 minutes + cooling & chilling

Here's a way you can create your own signature pickle or pepper without all the traditional pickling hassles. Add any variation of peppers you like. I often mix jalapeños and fresh Tabasco peppers but any variation will work. You can even remove the peppers for zero Scoville heat. But what fun would that be?

Infusing some heat in the pickles will make your guests remember the meal.

1 cup apple cider vinegar
1/3 cup sugar
1 clove garlic, minced
2 teaspoons lemon juice
1 teaspoon onion powder
1 teaspoon kosher salt
1 English cucumber, sliced
5-6 sweet mini peppers, sliced in thin rings
2 jalapenos, seeded and sliced in rings

1. In a medium saucepan over high heat, bring the apple cider vinegar and sugar to a boil, 3-4 minutes.
2. Stir in the garlic, lemon juice, onion powder, and salt, and continue cooking until the sugar and salt have dissolved, about 1 minute.
3. Divide the cucumbers, mini peppers and jalapenos into 3 pint-size Mason jars.
4. Pour the liquid over the vegetables and leave uncovered to cool completely, about 45 minutes.
5. Seal the jars and refrigerate overnight before serving.

 You can cut out all the pickling hassles by starting with inexpensive store bought pickles and doctoring them with your favorite sweetener and hot peppers. The sweet and heat will absorb and mellow after about a day of refrigeration. I experimented with different brands and prefer the crunchy snap of Vlasic Baby Kosher Dills, adding hot peppers and sugar.

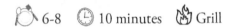

Fruit Kebabs with Prosciutto

6-8　　10 minutes　　Grill

The saltiness of cured meats and sweet fruit go great together. Use your favorite in-season firm-fleshed fruit. Pitted fruits are another great choice. It's the perfect summertime sweet grilled treat.

¼ cup olive oil
3 tablespoons molasses
1½ tablespoons apple cider vinegar
2 teaspoon Dijon mustard
2 teaspoon **Homemade Chili Powder** (*found in **Rubs & Pastes***)
1 teaspoon kosher salt
1 banana, cut into 1-inch pieces
1 cup strawberries, caps removed
1 cup pineapple chunks, cut in small wedges
1 firm peach, cut into wedges
1 mango, cut into chunks
6 ounces (12 thin slices) prosciutto

1. In a large bowl, whisk together olive oil, molasses, vinegar, mustard, Homemade Chili Powder, and salt until blended.
2. Add the cut fruit to the bowl and toss to coat.
3. Preheat the grill to medium-high heat (350°F-400°F).
4. Using metal skewers, thread the fruit in an alternating fashion, randomly adding in 2 pieces of prosciutto per skewer. Reserve the marinade for basting.
5. Place the kebabs on the grill grate and cook for 10 minutes, turning several times.
6. Remove from heat when lightly charred and baste the fruit with remaining marinade to serve.

 When you start prepping, give the metal skewers a brushing with a light, flavorless, oil. It will prevent the fruit from sticking to the skewers.

Breakfast Frittata

🕐 6   🕐 15 minutes   🔥 Grill

I love the smell of frittata in the morning. Smells like victory. Yes you can do breakfast on the grill. This is where the simplicity and dependability of a gas grill shines. What a way to wake up.

1 small sweet onion, chopped
½ cup chopped bell pepper
½ cup chopped tomato
8 eggs, beaten
¼ cup Half 'n Half
1 tablespoon minced garlic
2 teaspoons chopped fresh basil
1 teaspoon dried oregano
1 teaspoon salt
1 teaspoon freshly ground black pepper
¾ cup shredded cheddar cheese, divided
¼ cup shredded parmesan cheese, divided
1 tablespoon olive oil

1. Preheat the grill to medium (300°F-350°F).
2. In a large mixing bowl, combine chopped onion, bell pepper, tomato, eggs, Half 'n Half, garlic, basil, oregano, salt, and pepper.
3. In a separate small bowl, stir the cheddar cheese and parmesan cheese together. Reserve ½ cup of the combined cheeses for the topping.
4. Fold the remaining cheese into the vegetable mixture until well-combined.
5. Using a large cast iron skillet, add the olive oil and coat the pan.
6. Pour the vegetable egg mixture into the skillet, and top with the reserved cheeses.
7. Cover the skillet with aluminum foil and place it on the grill.
8. Grill the frittata with the lid closed for about 15 minutes until the eggs are set, but do not let it brown.
9. Remove it from the heat and serve immediately.

There is nothing better than the scent of breakfast on the grill and a chilled mimosa in your hand.

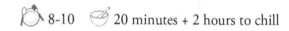

Saltine "Potato" Salad

8-10   20 minutes + 2 hours to chill

One of my favorite chefs of all time is the Cajun cook, Justin Wilson. I've always been a fan of his and of his humor. He has created a bunch of variations on this dish. This mock potato salad defies the senses as it tastes so familiar but really deserves a category all its own.

2 sleeves Saltine crackers, broken into large pieces
1 cup **Fridge Pickles & Peppers** (*found in this chapter*), or sweet pickle salad cubes
1 cup chopped celery
1 cup chopped onions
6 hard-boiled eggs, chopped
1 tablespoon Worcestershire sauce
2 teaspoons hot sauce
1 teaspoon freshly ground black pepper
1 cup chopped green onions
¾ - 1 cup mayonnaise, as needed

1. Add the cracker pieces to a large mixing bowl.
2. Drain and chop Fridge Pickles & Peppers (or drain sweet pickle salad cubes), and add to the bowl.
3. Gently stir in the celery, onions, hard-boiled eggs, Worcestershire sauce, hot sauce, black pepper, and green onions.
4. Fold in the mayonnaise, and chill for 2 hours before serving.

Try adding shrimp to this! Chop 2 cups peeled/deveined, cooked shrimp and toss with 1 tablespoon lime juice and 1 tablespoon Cajun seasoning. Top the above salad with the shrimp and chill as directed.

Subway Fatty

🔥 4   🕐 2 hours   🔥 Smoke   🪵 Oak

My friend and barbecue mentor, Jack Waiboer came up with this brilliant idea and deemed it the "Fat Guido Explosion" as a takeoff on the "bacon explosion" fatty that has taken over the internet. The concept is simple. Head to your favorite Subway restaurant and order up a "deconstructed" Italian sub - hold the lettuce. See my tip for the sub roll. Add a pound each of ground pork sausage and bacon, and you'll have everything you need to build this Italian-inspired feast.

1 pound ground sausage
3 teaspoons salt, divided
3 teaspoons freshly ground black pepper, divided
1 pound bacon (not thick sliced)
8 thin slices deli ham
8 slices Swiss cheese
2 tomatoes, thinly sliced
¼ cup sliced banana peppers
1 tablespoon olive oil
1 tablespoon balsamic vinegar
2 teaspoons chopped fresh oregano
2 teaspoons chopped fresh basil
1 teaspoon garlic powder
½ cup **Remoulade Burger Topping** *(found in **Top This**)*, or any marinara sauce

1. Preheat the smoker to 225°F and add wood.
2. Season the sausage with 1 teaspoon salt and 1 teaspoon pepper.
3. Lay out half of the bacon in vertical strips, side by side.
4. Lay the other half of the bacon horizontally over the bacon strips, and weave in an over under fashion, creating a tight square weave.
5. Spread the ground sausage over the bacon, completely covering it.
6. Layer the ham on top, then Swiss, then tomatoes over the whole fatty, leaving a 1-inch margin all the way around.
7. In a small bowl, whisk in oil, balsamic vinegar, oregano, basil, and garlic.
8. Sprinkle the banana peppers on top of the tomatoes, and season all over with the seasoned oil & vinegar.

9. From one side, roll the fatty up tightly and tuck in the bacon to secure.
10. Place the fatty on the smoker seam-side down, and smoke for 2 hours, or until a digital thermometer reaches 160°F.
11. Slice and serve with the Remoulade Burger Topping.

 If you kept the bread from Subway, grill it up in medallions and serve it on the side.

Grilled Garlic Bread Bruschetta

Makes 20   6 minutes   Grill

I love toasting thick slices of rustic breast on the grill. Just remember that bread can burn in the blink of an eye over direct heat. Keep a close eye and be ready to move each piece quickly to your serving platter to keep them from burning.

2 French bread baguettes
¼ cup olive oil
2 tablespoons minced garlic, divided
2 teaspoons kosher salt, divided
2 teaspoons freshly ground black pepper, divided
6 Roma tomatoes, chopped
1 small red onion, chopped
1 tablespoon chopped fresh basil
1 tablespoon dried oregano
1 tablespoon red wine vinegar
½ cup shredded Parmesan cheese

1. Preheat grill to medium-high heat (350°F-400°F).
2. Slice the baguettes on an angle (½ inch thick), about 20 slices.
3. In a small bowl, whisk together olive oil, 1 tablespoon garlic, 1 teaspoon salt, and 1 teaspoon pepper.
4. Baste both sides of each slice with the seasoned olive oil.
5. Place the bread on the grill for 3 minutes on one side only, and remove from the heat.
6. In a medium bowl combine tomatoes, onions, basil, oregano, red wine vinegar, remaining garlic, remaining salt, and remaining pepper.
7. Flip the bread slices, and top the grilled side with the mixture.
8. Gently place the bread slices back on the grill.
9. Grill for 3 minutes, top with Parmesan cheese, and serve immediately.

 Try this sweet variation. Baste the bread slices with butter and grill. Spread a thin layer of peanut butter on the bread slices, and top with sliced strawberries and whipped cream to serve.

Skillet Biscuits

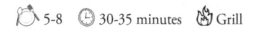 5-8   🕐 30-35 minutes   🔥 Grill

Every once in a while your barbecue will require some heavy lifting. You'll get your workout here by using a heavy, well seasoned, cast iron skillet. Like I said, heavy lifting. Enjoy the carbs; you've earned it!

1 cup (2 sticks) + 3 tablespoons unsalted butter, divided
4 cups self-rising flour
1 tablespoon sugar
1½ teaspoons kosher salt
1½ cups buttermilk
3 tablespoons honey, for serving

1. Preheat the grill to medium-high heat (350°F-400°F).
2. Make sure the butter is cold, and slice the 2 sticks into 16 tablespoons.
3. Using a mixer, combine flour, the 16 tablespoons of butter, sugar, and salt, until crumbly.
4. Add buttermilk and working on a lightly floured surface, roll the dough into a ball, kneading several times.
5. Place 1 tablespoon of butter in a cast iron skillet. Set it on the grill to melt.
6. Divide the dough into 10 even balls and place them in the cast iron skillet.
7. Melt 1 tablespoon of butter and baste the tops of the biscuits.
8. Place the skillet on the grill and cook for 30-35 minutes.
9. Remove from the heat, baste with the remaining tablespoon of butter, and drizzle with honey to serve.

 For a savory variation, try adding ½ cup shredded cheddar cheese to the flour mixture, and 1 teaspoon of garlic powder to the basting butter.

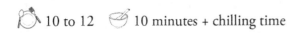

White Banana Pudding

🍶 10 to 12   🥣 10 minutes + chilling time

Banana pudding is the ultimate Southern barbecue dessert. Don't settle for the yellow, phony, fake banana flavor from the little square box mix. The heavy whipping cream will keep this authentic pudding's appearance more white than yellow. It's the tell-tale sign of the real deal.

1 (14-ounce) can sweetened condensed milk
1 ½ cups ice water
1 (3.4-ounce) box vanilla instant pudding mix
3 cups heavy whipping cream
4 cups sliced bananas, sprinkled with 2 tablespoons lemon juice
1 (12-ounce) box vanilla wafers

1. In a large bowl, beat the sweetened condensed milk and the water until completely blended.
2. Add in the dry vanilla pudding mix, and stir until well-combined.
3. Cover the bowl with plastic wrap and refrigerate for 4 hours.
4. In a medium bowl, beat the heavy cream until stiff peaks start to form.
5. Gradually fold the whipped cream into the pudding, and mix well.
6. Assemble using a trifle bowl, layering 1/3 of the vanilla wafers overlapping on the bottom, then 1/3 of the bananas, and topping with 1/3 of the pudding.
7. Repeat two more times, reserving a few vanilla wafers to place on the top layer.
8. Cover tightly with plastic wrap and chill in the refrigerator for 1 hour before serving.

 Bananas will start to turn after about 8 hours, even if using lemon juice. It is best to use bananas that are still a little green for this recipe, as ripe bananas will turn brown faster.

Roasted Pear Crostini

🍳 Serves 4-5   🕐 10 minutes   🔥 Grill

Fresh pears make this dish a summertime delight. Look for pears with firm flesh that will hold up well on the grill. The grilling will bring out their inherent sweetness. If you can't find perfect pears in the regular produce section check for fresher options in the organic section. It can be worth paying extra for the perfect pear.

3 pears, halved and cored
¼ cup (½ stick) unsalted butter, melted
1 tablespoon firmly packed light brown sugar
1 teaspoon kosher salt
1 teaspoon freshly ground black pepper
1 French bread baguette, sliced into about 10 (½-inch) slices
1 tablespoon olive oil
3 cloves garlic, minced
4 slices **Grilled Butterscotch Bacon**, *(found in **Pork**)*, cooked & crumbled
½ cup **Seasoned Smoked Pecans**, *(found in this chapter)*, chopped
¼ cup Bleu cheese crumbles
1 tablespoon balsamic vinegar
1 tablespoon honey
¼ cup chopped green onions

1. Preheat the grill to medium heat (300°F-350°F).
2. In a small bowl, combine the butter, brown sugar, salt, and pepper.
3. Spread the butter on the cut side of the pears and place them on the grill, cut-side down.
4. Grill for 5-10 minutes, until softened and grill marks have formed.
5. Remove pears from the heat and let cool before chopping.
6. In a small bowl, whisk together olive oil and garlic.
7. Baste both sides of the bread with the olive oil and garlic, and place the bread on the grill.
8. Grill one side of the bread only for 3 minutes and remove from the heat.
9. In a medium bowl, combine the chopped bacon, pecans, and Bleu cheese.
10. Flip the crostini over and top the grilled side with the mixture before returning to the grill.

11. Continue grilling for 3 minutes.
12. In a small bowl, whisk together balsamic vinegar and honey.
13. To serve, top with green onions and drizzle with balsamic vinegar and honey.

 For a variation, try this with green apples instead of pears.

Grit Cakes

🥄 Makes 48 mini grit cakes   🕐 1 hour + 15 minutes   🔥 Oven

You could cook these grit cakes on a dependable gas grill, but it's not a dish that benefits much from the grill. Keep it easy in the oven and save the grill real estate for the main dish.

2 (14-ounce) cans chicken broth
1½ cups Half 'n Half, divided
1½ cups white grits, quick-cooking
1 cup grated Parmesan cheese
½ cup sour cream
3 tablespoons butter
1 teaspoon salt

1. In a large Dutch oven over medium-high heat, bring the chicken broth and Half 'n Half to a boil.
2. Stir in the grits and bring it back up to a boil.
3. Reduce the heat to low, cover, and simmer for about 5 minutes, stirring often.
4. Remove from the heat and stir in the Parmesan cheese, sour cream, butter, and salt.
5. Grease a large jellyroll pan and pour the grits into the prepared pan. Spread evenly.
6. Cover with plastic wrap and refrigerate overnight.
7. Preheat the oven to 400°F.
8. Turn out the grits onto a cutting surface and using a mini biscuit cutter, cut mini circles out of the grits. About 48
9. Place the mini grit cakes on a baking sheet covered in parchment paper.
10. Bake the grit cakes for 15 minutes, flip and bake for 45 more minutes.
11. Remove from the heat and let cool.

Serve topped with chopped sautéed shrimp in Alfredo sauce, or pulled pork in barbecue sauce, as a satisfying appetizer.

CHAPTER 10

SIDE NOTES VEGETABLES, SALADS & SIDE DISHES

*"Last night I had a typical cholesterol-free dinner:
baked squash, skimmed milk, and gelatin.
I'm sure this will not make me live any longer,
but I know it's going to seem longer."*
—Groucho Marx

Vegetables aren't just for health nuts anymore. They're great on the grill and add variety to your grilling life. I'm not sure where I heard this, but did you know the word vegetarian is an ancient word originally translated as "bad hunter?"

Veggies open up a whole wide world of flavors and textures to add to your outdoor cooking. To some, corn on the cob is a barbecue staple. To others, Coleslaw and potato salad are a must.

Best Veggies

What's cool about vegetables is that you can grill them sliced, diced, and even whole. We will smoke a whole cabbage head in the recipes here. You can score the skin of eggplant and smoke it for the key ingredient in an exotic Baba ganoush. Just look for vegetables with a firm flesh that will absorb smoke flavors.

Cabbage and cauliflower "steaks" cut from the stalk to the top as half-inch thick disks are a spectacular blank canvas for zesty sauces and marinades.

Once these slabs start to brown you can baste them with butter and salt and drain them on paper towels. Have fun experimenting with the sauces at the end of the grilling time.

I like using buffalo wing sauce on purple cabbage steaks. Then top them with Bleu cheese crumbles. Sliced Swiss, or shredded cheddar, for a satisfying, and meat-free side. Get colorful and mix it up with green cabbage, and purple cauliflower "steaks" for visual variety.

Salads

Many salads we eat with barbecue are mayonnaise-based, "wet" salads, like coleslaw and potato salad. But you can also grill lettuce. Use cold halves of romaine or iceberg wedges, and give the surface a slight char over quick high heat to add flavor without cooking the entire head of delicate leaves. Of course, you can also enjoy a "meat lovers" salad, bringing it back to the barbecue world, by simply topping a traditional salad with strips or chunks of grilled meat.

What Kind of Side Dishes Will We Be Enjoying?

Even Cartman from South Park, knows you need a few sides…even if you're just serving frozen waffles. In barbecue, the most popular side dishes range from macaroni and cheese to hush puppies.

What is the most popular barbecue side dish in America? Some would argue you can't serve barbecue without baked beans, Coleslaw, mac and cheese, potato salad, or even hush puppies! After a bit of research, I think the blue ribbon may just go to mac and cheese. It is the most viewed of all the recipes on The Food Network's website. Plus, according to the American Cheese Society, macaroni and cheese has remained on America's top ten comfort foods for decades. In any given 12-week period, approximately one-third of the American population will eat macaroni and cheese at least once. If you are looking for a crowd-pleaser – go with mac and cheese.

Look for two great options in the free Sauces and Sides book on my website, or try my **Piggy Mac** *(found in **Pork** in this book).*

Vegetable Tricks

Sure they are healthy, but vegetables are also delicious when kissed with fire on the grill. Here are a few of my best *Veggie Tricks:*

- **Basket case.** A grill basket can help you keep sliced or diced vegetables from falling through the grate and still easily give you the heat and smoke to cook the food to perfection. This is similar to a flat grill mat, but they are basket-shaped and can withstand the high heat required to brown. Zucchini and onions with a flavorful marinade make for a quick zesty dish helped by a good grill basket. Toss or stir the mix with seasonings for even more flavor.
- **Tater Tip. Need a quick way to peel a potato?** Score your potato around the center with a knife before boiling 15 minutes. Then plunge in a bowl of ice water until cool enough to handle. The skin should slip off easily!
- **Tater Tip Two.** You can accelerate the cooking of your baked potato by inserting a clean long aluminum nail lengthwise into the spud's center. The metal will transfer the heat more quickly to the middle. Avoid galvanized, chemically treated, or coated nails.
- **Garlic on the side.** If you're smoking anything over wood or charcoal, try this trick to add extra flavor. Just toss a few large cloves of garlic on the hot coals. It will infuse lighter meats and vegetables with a subtle garlic flavor.
- **Soak for moisture.** If you have tender vegetables you plan to grill hot and fast, you can soak them in water for thirty minutes to keep them from drying out too quickly.
- **When you're hot, you're hot.** You can tame the heat of hot peppers and chilies by removing the seeds and white internal "membrane" of the peppers. This will dramatically lower the spicy heat and the peppers will retain all of their flavor.
- **Appeal of the peel.** You can keep skinned veggies from drying out and/or losing their shape by leaving their skin intact. This works great for squash and especially eggplant slices.
- **Stick it to 'em.** Vegetables offer great variety for kebab skewers. Oil the skewers before cooking to prevent pieces from sticking. You can also cook each individual vegetable type on separate skewers to adapt to the veggie's differing cook times.

- **Icy heat.** You may think frozen veggies are off-limits in barbecue, but on the rare occasion, it can be a tricky time saver. You can use skin-on diced frozen potatoes (par-boiled) to whip up a rustic potato salad in an instant.
- **Cut the tears.** You can minimize the tears associated with slicing onions by simply submerging the peeled onions in water prior to cutting. You can also try wearing swim goggles, removing the core first, or holding a piece of bread in your mouth, but this is by far the least embarrassing.
- **Onion second half.** If you need only one half of a fresh onion to store in the refrigerator, use the top half to cook with first. The onion's bottom "root end" will keep fresh much longer, stored in the refrigerator.
- **Peeling Peppers.** One trick for peeling peppers works in perfect harmony with the world of barbecue. Fire roast your green or red bell peppers directly on high heat, or directly on the coals until they blacken and blister. Then, wrap them loosely inside a paper bag for a few minutes to allow them to continue to cook and steam off the fire in the bag. In about five minutes, you'll be able to use the light grip of the bag's paper to squeeze and peel them right out of the mouth of the bag. You may still have a few black bits to pick off, but it will make your peeling much more appeal-ing.

- **Corny situation**. Want your grilled corn *off* the cob? Here's how you can cut and keep those kernels from scattering. Use the hole in the center of an ordinary bundt cake pan to brace your corn cob. As you push it through, the kernels will fall neatly into the pan.
- **Easy corn silk removal.** If you can't stand the hassle of picking tiny silks from your corn cobs, try this hack. Slice off the stem end of each cob and microwave your corn for 4 minutes per ear. Use oven mitts to then grip the top end with the silks and squeeze the cob out cleanly. It's almost like squeezing the last bit of toothpaste out of the tube. It works every time!
- **Organic trick.** If you don't have time to wait for fruit or vegetables to ripen, do a quick check of the organic section of the grocery. I don't always like the extra cost added to organic, but if you need it now (often with avocados), it's worth the price for organic. I remember when we used to lick stamps? Was that organic?
- **Steak out.** You can cut steaks from a few vegetables known as cruciferous vegetables. These varieties of healthy vegetables are known for their thick stalks, such as cauliflower, broccoli, and cabbage. Cut steaks from the whole large heads by slicing down along the stalks. Use a sharp knife, trim them with the stem up, and reserve the trimmings for other recipes. There will be plenty of quality scraps, but you should be able to fashion two to three slices with enough firm stem intact to hold them together on the grill.

Grillustration: **Cauliflower Steaks**

SIDE NOTES RECIPES

Quick Southern Potato Salad
Crispy Brussels Sprouts
Braised Cabbage Head
Sweet Slaw
Mexican Street Corn
Grilled Wedge
Baked Ranch Potatoes
Skillet Cornbread Salad
Inverted Onion Tarte
Roasted Parmesan Squash, Zucchini & Onions
Summer Salad
Baked Beans
Cinnamon Sugar Sweet Potato Fries
Grilled Parmesan Onions
Corn Pudding

Quick Southern Potato Salad

 8   🥣 20 minutes

People have very personal preferences with potato salad. Some insist you can only use "new red potatoes" for good potato salad. Others will debate skin on or skin off. I love it all, but decided to cut down on the prep time and decision making by going frozen.

The trick here is using prepackaged and diced frozen potatoes. They're intended for serving as "hash browns," but, in our house, they're not just for breakfast anymore.

1 (2-pound) bag frozen diced hash brown potatoes
2 tablespoons water
½-1 cup mayonnaise, as needed
½ cup sour cream
½ cup sweet pickle salad cubes, well-drained
¼ cup mustard
1 bouillon cube, crushed (or 1 teaspoon poultry seasoning)
2 teaspoons salt
1½ teaspoons freshly ground black pepper
1½ teaspoons garlic powder
½ cup chopped celery
½ cup chopped green onions
8 slices bacon, cooked crispy and crumbled (reserve 1 tablespoon bacon grease)
4 hard-boiled eggs, chopped

1. Place frozen diced potatoes into a large microwaveable bowl with water, and microwave for 4 minutes.
2. Stir the potatoes and microwave for 4 more minutes. Set aside to cool.
3. In a large bowl, whisk together mayonnaise, sour cream, pickle cubes, mustard, bouillon or poultry seasoning, salt, pepper, garlic powder, celery, and green onions.
4. Add in the crumbled bacon, warm (not solid) bacon grease, and chopped hard-boiled eggs, until well-combined.

5. Gently fold in the cooked potatoes.
6. Chill at least 2-3 hours before serving.

 Using fresh potatoes instead? You can help keep them from sprouting in storage by placing a piece of fresh ginger root, or half an apple, in the bag with them.

Crispy Brussels Sprouts

🥘 4   🕐 15 minutes   🔥 Air Fryer

Did you know that Brussels sprouts were named after the capital of Belgium? It's true. But they've been in America since the 1800's. I always thought of them as an "old fashioned" veggie and didn't care for them much until I tried them fried crispy. It is possible to do this in a pan, or deep fryer, but this is the real reason I think you need an air fryer. They're nice and crispy with this device.

2 tablespoons olive oil
1 teaspoon kosher salt
1 teaspoon freshly ground black pepper
1 teaspoon garlic powder
1 pound Brussels sprouts, ends removed and sliced
1 tablespoon balsamic vinegar
1 tablespoon shredded Parmesan cheese, for serving

1. In a medium bowl, whisk together olive oil, salt, pepper, and garlic powder.
2. Toss the sliced Brussels sprouts to coat well, and let stand in the refrigerator for 1 hour.
3. Pour the marinated Brussels sprouts into the air fryer and set on 375°F.
4. Cook for 15 minutes until crispy and slightly charred.
5. Toss the cooked sprouts into a serving bowl, drizzle with the balsamic vinegar, and sprinkle with the Parmesan cheese to serve.

 Shop for same sized Brussels sprouts and cut them into even slices. The dense larger pieces tend to take longer to cook. For best results you'll want everything to cook, and crisp up, evenly. Toss in the leaves that randomly fall off during slicing in the fryer as well. These will be extra crispy delicious additions!

Braised Cabbage Head

🍽 6-8   🕐 1 hour   🔥 Grill

Typically braising is done with meat. It's also not really in the world of barbecue. But it's a cooking method that works perfectly with this hearty vegetable side dish. Because the cabbage is 91% water, it can take a lot of heat and hold its moisture.

Not only does it taste fantastic, it's affordable, and a macho show stopper on the grill. Who says cabbage ain't cool!

4 slices bacon
1 fresh cabbage head
¼ cup (½ stick) butter, softened
3 chicken bouillon cubes
2 teaspoons freshly ground black pepper
½ cup grated Parmesan cheese

1. Cook the bacon halfway (about 3 minutes in the microwave).
2. Let cool and chop the bacon.
3. Preheat the grill to medium- high heat (350°F - 400°F).
4. Core the cabbage completely from the stem end. This will create a deep hole that you can stuff.
5. Smear the butter all over the inside of the cored-out cabbage head.
6. Add the bouillon cubes, bacon pieces, and pepper.
7. Wrap the cabbage in aluminum foil, leaving only the hole at the top exposed.
8. Place the cabbage on the grill with the exposed part up. Use a ring of crumpled foil to stabilize.
9. Close the lid and grill the cabbage head for 1 hour.
10. Pour the contents of the cavity into a large bowl, and chop the cabbage head.
11. Add the cabbage pieces to the bowl and toss to coat.
12. Pour onto a serving platter and sprinkle with the Parmesan cheese to serve.

 Cabbage heads can last up to two weeks in the refrigerator and sealed in a plastic bag.

Sweet Slaw

🕐 8-10   🕐 20 minutes + marinating & chilling time

My favorite barbecue side dish is Cole slaw. I don't know why, but I love the combination of crunch and sweetness. The name for Cole Slaw is interesting. Its origins are not about "cold" but from the Dutch translation of "koolsla" for cabbage salad. I do however suggest serving it nice and cold.

1 head cabbage, shredded
1 carrot, shredded
1 cup sugar
½ cup cold water
½ cup vinegar
1 teaspoon salt
1 teaspoon pepper
8 ounces heavy whipping cream
1 tablespoon paprika

1. In a large mixing bowl, combine the cabbage, carrot, sugar, cold water, vinegar, salt, and pepper.
2. Refrigerate a minimum of 3 hours up to overnight.
3. Drain the liquid and stir in the heavy cream (do not whip).
4. Refrigerate for 30 minutes – 1 hour, and sprinkle with paprika to serve.

 There are many slaw recipes out there to try, from mayonnaise-based to vinegar-based, sweet, savory, and Asian, you name it. Try replacing the heavy whipping cream, water, and sugar in this recipe with ¼ cup olive oil, 1 tablespoon grainy mustard, and 1 teaspoon celery seed, for a more savory slaw variation.

Mexican Street Corn

🔥 6   🕐 10-15 minutes   🔥 Grill

Growing up, corn on the cob has always seemed like a North American dish. However, now that I'm fully grown I can't think of corn on the cob without thinking of Elote. It's the Mexican word for an ear of corn on or off the plant. They do it right in Central America where, in some places, they even have "eloteros" who sell the street corn from a cart.

Here's a recipe to help you to be an eloteros in your own backyard.

¼ cup mayonnaise
¼ cup sour cream
2 cloves garlic, minced
¼ cup **Citrus Chile Butter Paste** *(found in **Rubs & Pastes**)*, melted
6 ears fresh corn, husks on
½ cup Parmesan cheese
2 teaspoon ground chipotle powder
1 teaspoon ground cumin
1 teaspoon onion powder
1 teaspoon kosher salt
2 tablespoon lime juice
2 tablespoons chopped fresh cilantro, for serving

1. Preheat grill to medium-high heat (350°F - 400°F).
2. In a medium bowl, combine mayonnaise, sour cream, and garlic. Set aside.
3. Pull the husks back on the corn but do not remove.
4. Remove the silks and baste the corn with Citrus Chile Butter Paste.
5. Replace the husks, and place the corn on the grill grate.
6. Grill for 10-15 minutes, turning often.
7. Remove the corn from the heat and remove the husks.
8. Slather the corn with the mayonnaise mixture.
9. In a medium bowl, combine the Parmesan cheese, chipotle powder, ground cumin, onion powder, and salt.

10. Dredge the corn through the seasoned Parmesan cheese.
11. Place the hot corn on a serving platter and sprinkle with lime juice and cilantro to serve.

 To serve this off the cob, add 4½ - 5 cups corn kernels to a large bowl and stir in the remaining ingredients from above. Bake @ 350ºF for 30 minutes until bubbly, and serve hot.

Grilled Wedge

🗲 4   🕐 1-2 minutes   🔥 Grill

Serving your salad in the form of a grilled wedge transforms your lettuce from rabbit food to a hearty side. The trick to grilling salad is to start with chilled, firm heads of lettuce, and add a searing hot grill. You don't want to cook the lettuce; you just want to give the edges a bit of char.

½ cup olive oil
½ cup balsamic vinegar
2 teaspoons mustard
2 teaspoons honey
1 teaspoon dried basil
½ teaspoon kosher salt
½ teaspoon freshly ground black pepper
1 head of iceberg lettuce, cold
1 large tomato, diced
6 slices bacon, cooked crispy and crumbled
½ cup Bleu cheese crumbles
¼ cup chopped bell pepper
2 tablespoons chopped red onions
¼ cup **Seasoned Smoked Pecans** (*found in **Nuts, Cheese, Desserts & More***), chopped

1. In a small bowl, whisk together olive oil, balsamic vinegar, mustard, honey, basil, salt, and pepper to make a vinaigrette dressing. Reserve half for serving.
2. Preheat the grill to medium-high heat (350°F - 400°F).
3. Cut the head of lettuce into 4 wedges, but do not remove the core.
4. Baste each cold wedge with the remaining vinaigrette and place on the grill, cut side down.
5. Sear the lettuce wedges for 1-2 minutes, until they have good grill marks.
6. Remove from the heat and cut out the core.
7. Refrigerate the wedges until ready to serve.

8. Plate the wedges and sprinkle the tomato, bacon, Bleu cheese, bell pepper, red onions, and chopped Seasoned Smoked Pecans over all.
9. Drizzle with the reserved vinaigrette dressing to serve.

 Other heads of lettuce that also work well on the grill are radicchio and tight heads of romaine. Split lengthwise.

Baked Ranch Potatoes

🍳 12   🕐 1 hour   🔥 Oven

We use "new potatoes" in this recipe because new potatoes tend to hold up a bit better in the refrigerator as well as being stirred about in a hot mixture. Old potatoes, such as Idaho or Russets, are larger, drier and have more starch so they are better suited for French fries and baking whole.

2 tablespoons unsalted butter, melted
1 tablespoon kosher salt
2 teaspoons freshly ground black pepper
2 teaspoons garlic powder
2 teaspoons onion powder
5 pounds red potatoes, washed & cut in quarters
1 medium onion, diced
2 bell peppers, diced
6 slices bacon, cooked & coarsely chopped, divided (reserve 1 tablespoon bacon grease)
1 cup shredded cheddar cheese, divided
½ cup shredded Parmesan cheese, divided
¼ cup (½ stick) butter, cut in 8 pieces
1/3 cup bottled Ranch dressing

1. Preheat the oven to 400°F.
2. In a small bowl, stir together melted butter, salt, pepper, garlic powder, and onion powder.
3. Place the potatoes in a large bowl and add the seasoned butter. Toss to coat.
4. Using a baking sheet lined with parchment paper, spread out the potatoes in a single layer.
5. Place on the center rack in the oven and bake for 30 minutes.
6. In a medium bowl, combine the onion, peppers, bacon, and bacon grease until blended.
7. Increase the heat to broil for 5 minutes, and remove the potatoes from the heat.
8. Reduce the oven heat to 350°F.
9. Spray 9x13 baking dish with cooking spray and pour in half the potatoes.
10. Top with half the vegetable and bacon mixture and spread evenly.
11. Sprinkle ½ cup cheddar cheese over all.

12. Repeat the layers, adding the remaining potatoes, then the vegetable and bacon mixture, and topping with the remaining cheddar cheese.
13. Sprinkle the Parmesan cheese over all and dot the butter around and through the potatoes.
14. Drizzle the Ranch dressing over the top and place the casserole back in the oven.
15. Roast for 30 minutes and serve warm.

 For a low carb variation, try replacing the baked potatoes with chopped, cooked cauliflower. It becomes much lighter, yet still delicious.

Skillet Cornbread Salad

🧅 20   🕐 45 minutes – 1 hour   🔥 Grill

I use a skillet to help bake up the cornbread for this chunky layered cowboy salad.

The great thing about a cast iron skillet is that they can act as an extension of your grill. Just remember to plan for some extra time to allow the cast iron to warm up. Always have a hot mat and oven mitts, or gloves nearby.

¼ cup (½ stick) unsalted butter, divided
1½ cups yellow cornmeal
½ cup all-purpose flour
1 tablespoon baking powder
2 teaspoons kosher salt
1½ cups buttermilk
2 eggs, beaten
2 cups packed, torn romaine lettuce, divided
2 stalks celery, chopped, divided
1 tomato, chopped, divided
1 bell pepper, chopped, divided
1 red onion, chopped, divided
1 can pinto beans, drained, divided
1 can sweet corn kernels, drained, divided
2 cup shredded cheddar cheese, divided
8 slices bacon, cooked & crumbled, divided
1 (1-ounce) package dry Ranch salad dressing mix
1 (16-ounce) sour cream
1 cup mayonnaise

1. Preheat the grill to medium heat (300°F-350°F).
2. Place 2 tablespoons butter in a cast iron skillet on the grill and melt.
3. In a medium bowl, whisk together cornmeal, flour, baking powder, and salt.
4. Add in buttermilk, remaining butter, and eggs, and pour the batter into the hot skillet.
5. Place on the grill for 45 minutes - 1 hour, until bread is lightly browned, and a toothpick inserted into the center comes out clean. Let cool.

6. Crumble the cooled cornbread and layer half in the bottom of a large trifle bowl.
7. In layers, top with ½ the lettuce, ½ the celery, ½ the tomato, ½ the bell pepper, ½ the red onion, ½ the beans, ½ the corn, ½ the cheddar cheese, and ½ the crumbled bacon.
8. In a medium bowl, whisk together the dry Ranch dressing mix, sour cream, and mayonnaise. Top the salad with ½ the dressing.
9. Add the remaining crumbled cornbread and repeat the layers, adding the remaining lettuce, remaining celery, remaining tomato, remaining bell pepper, remaining onion, remaining beans, remaining corn, remaining cheese, remaining bacon, and remaining dressing. Cover and chill for 2 hours before serving.

 If under a time crunch, try substituting 1 (8½-ounce) box of corn muffin mix prepared by package directions, for the cornbread.

Inverted Onion Tarte

🍳 3-4   🕐 30-35 minutes   🔥 Grill

This is the kind of dish that most people would reserve for the kitchen oven. However, if you have a dependable gas or pellet grill, it can be a fun challenge for outdoor cooking. You'll want to be able to really maintain a steady temperature. If you're cooking during the summer months it helps to cook outside and lighten the load on the air conditioning inside.

3 sweet onions
¼ cup (½ stick) unsalted butter
2 tablespoons honey
2 tablespoons balsamic vinegar
2 cloves garlic, minced
1 tablespoon dried thyme
¼ teaspoon kosher salt
¼ teaspoon freshly ground black pepper
¼ cup grated Parmesan cheese
1 refrigerated puff pastry (if frozen, thaw), cut into a 13" circle
Egg wash: 1 beaten egg + 1 tablespoon water mixed

1. Preheat grill to medium-high heat (350°F - 400°F).
2. Cut the peeled onions lengthwise into small wedges.
3. Drop the butter into a 12-inch cast iron skillet and place on the grill to melt.
4. Add the onions to the skillet and sauté for 5 minutes until translucent and starting to brown.
5. Stir in the honey, balsamic vinegar, and garlic. Continue cooking another 5 minutes.
6. Sprinkle the thyme, salt, pepper, and Parmesan cheese over the onions.
7. Carefully lay the puff pastry circle over the onions and tuck the edges down toward the skillet.
8. Brush the pastry with the egg wash and cut 4 small slits to allow the steam to escape.
9. Close the lid and allow it to cook for 20-25 minutes until browned.
10. Invert the tarte onto a large platter and serve immediately.

Roasted Parmesan Squash, Zucchini & Onions

6   20-30 minutes   Grill

Squash and zucchini are great summertime grilling subjects but they can be a hassle to keep from falling through the grill's grates. Often I'll use a grill basket or "wok" to keep everything contained neatly on the grill and still allow for browning and char. Creating foil pouches like, we do here, is another easy option.

2 yellow squash
2 zucchini
1 large onion
½ cup **Citrus Chile Butter Paste** *(found in **Rubs & Pastes**)*, melted

1. Preheat the grill to medium high heat (350°F - 400°F).
2. Slice the squash, zucchini, and onions, and place into a large bowl.
3. Add the Citrus Chile Butter Paste and toss to coat.
4. Using heavy duty aluminum foil cut 6 pieces that are 12 inches long.
5. Spray one side of the foil pieces with cooking spray.
6. Divide the vegetable mixture by six, and place on the cooking spray side of each packet.
7. Fold the packets to completely seal and place on the grill, seam-side up.
8. Grill the packets about 20-30 minutes until the vegetables are to desired tenderness.

 Feel free to change up the veggies in this easy side dish. Peppers, potatoes, mushrooms, green beans, and even hamburger patties work well, too.

Summer Salad

 8   🥣 15 minutes

You know you're more than 80% through with a barbecue book when you hit a *second* salad recipe! Seriously, I've been trying to stick to a Keto diet lately and I love this salad. Plus, barbecue and keto dieting go great together. The hardest part about this salad is timing the avocado for ripeness!

4 Roma tomatoes, cut into wedges
1 cucumber, cut into 1-inch cubes
1 red onion, coarsely chopped
4 tablespoons chopped fresh cilantro
2 cloves garlic, minced
2 tablespoons lime juice, divided
2 tablespoons olive oil
1 teaspoon kosher salt
1 teaspoon freshly ground black pepper
3 ripe avocados

1. In a large bowl, add tomato, cucumber, onion, cilantro, garlic, 1 tablespoon lime juice, olive oil, salt, and pepper.
2. Stir to coat and refrigerate for at least 1 hour to chill.
3. Just before serving, cut avocados into wedges and sprinkle with the remaining lime juice.
4. Gently fold avocados into the salad and serve immediately.

 Looking for the ripest avocados at the grocery store? This is one time when paying more in the "organic section" may be worth it. With avocado, ripeness timing is everything.

Baked Beans

🕳 10-12   🕐 1½ hours   🔥 Smoker   🪵 Hickory

Baked beans are sort of like barbecue sauces. With so many great commercial varieties available in stores it is fun to use your favorite store brand as a starting point, and, as a blank canvas to embellish with your own favorite flavors. Here is a look at how my wife MJ and I doctor them. Of course it starts with bacon...

6 slices of bacon
2 (28-ounce) cans baked beans
1 bell pepper, chopped
2 tablespoons mustard
2 tablespoons ketchup
2 tablespoons molasses
1 tablespoon minced garlic
1 small onion, chopped

1. Preheat the smoker to 225°F and add wood.
2. Cook the bacon in the microwave for 3 minutes, to partially cook, and cut into large chunks.
3. Using a disposable aluminum pan with high sides, pour in the beans.
4. Stir in the bacon, bell pepper, mustard, ketchup, molasses, and minced garlic.
5. Place the pan on the smoker rack and smoke for 1 hour.
6. Stir in the onion and continue smoking for 30 more minutes until bubbly and sticky.
7. Remove the beans from the heat and serve hot.

 If you have leftover pulled pork or brisket, try adding 1 cup to the baked beans before baking, for a hearty side dish.

Cinnamon Sugar Sweet Potato Fries

🍅 12   🕐 30-35 minutes   🔥 Oven

Sweet potatoes are packed with nutrients and they are naturally sweet. But the brown sugar and cinnamon we add here really amps-up the sweetness.

6 pounds (6-8) sweet potatoes, washed
¼ cup olive oil
4 tablespoons cornstarch
2 teaspoons kosher salt
1 tablespoon firmly packed brown sugar
1 teaspoon ground cinnamon
½ teaspoon cayenne pepper

1. Preheat the oven to 425°F.
2. Line 2 baking sheets with parchment paper, and spray with cooking spray.
3. Roughly peel the potatoes and cut them into ¼-inch sticks. (Some skin on the potatoes is fine.)
4. Place the fries in a large bowl and add the olive oil. Toss to lightly coat.
5. Divide the fries between the two pans in a single layer for even baking.
6. Sprinkle the cornstarch over the fries and roll around a little to try to coat evenly.
7. Sprinkle the fries with the salt and place the pans in the oven.
8. Using the center and bottom racks, bake for 20 minutes. (The top rack is too close to the heating element and could burn the fries before they finish cooking.)
9. In a small bowl, mix the brown sugar, cinnamon, and cayenne pepper.
10. Flip the fries over, and reverse the pans on the oven racks.
11. Bake for 10-15 more minutes, keeping a close watch as they can burn easily. Remove the fries from the heat when they have a matte, crispy finish and the edges are slightly charred.
12. Sprinkle the fries immediately with the brown sugar mixture, and serve warm.

 To enhance browning of your fries, pat the sweet potatoes dry before baking.

Grilled Parmesan Onions

🕐 4   🕙 1-1 ½ hours   🔥 Smoke   🪵 Mesquite

These onion "bombs" bring the flavor to any grill, smoker, or even a camp fire. They're hard to "screw-up" as they are very resilient to high heat and have incredible flavor.

You can use standard sweet onions here. However, I always try to find true Vidalia onions if I can. The sandy Georgia soil and climate really give them better flavor.

4 large Vidalia onions, peeled
½ cup (1 stick) butter, divided
4 chicken bouillon cubes
1 cup grated Parmesan cheese

1. Preheat smoker to 275°F and add wood.
2. Using a paring knife inserted at an angle from the top, cut all the way around, and remove the top. Hollow out the inside about halfway down into the onion.
3. Smear 2 tablespoons of butter down into the center of each onion and up the insides.
4. Place the bouillon cubes down into the onions, and top each with ¼ cup Parmesan cheese.
5. Replace the tops on the onions and wrap each tightly up the sides in a separate piece of aluminum foil, but leave the tops uncovered to let the smoke permeate the flavor.
6. Put the onions in a baking pan and place it on the smoker rack and smoke for 1-1½ hours, until the onions are tender to the touch.
7. Remove the foil and serve immediately.

Corn Pudding

🍳 15-20   🕐 1 hour + 15 minutes   🔥 Oven

This is called a pudding but is has more casserole or soufflé texture, like a bread pudding. It is a satisfying, and hearty way to enjoy your vegetables. Prepare for carb overload.

1 pound frozen white whole kernel corn, thawed
1 (20-ounce) tube frozen white creamed corn, thawed
1 butter cake mix, dry
1 box corn muffin mix, dry
1 cup shredded cheddar cheese
1 cup buttermilk
1 cup (2 sticks) butter, melted
4 eggs, beaten
1 teaspoon vanilla
1 tablespoon kosher salt
24 ounces sour cream
1 tablespoon honey

1. Preheat oven to 350°F.
2. Spray a large ½-size aluminum foil deep steam table pan (extra deep 9"x13") with cooking spray.
3. In a large bowl, add whole kernel corn, creamed corn, cake mix, corn muffin mix, cheddar cheese, buttermilk, melted butter, eggs, vanilla, and salt.
4. Mix until well-blended and then gently fold in the sour cream.
5. Pour the corn pudding into the prepared baking dish and cover with aluminum foil.
6. Place the baking dish in the oven on the center rack and bake covered for 45 minutes.
7. Remove the aluminum foil and continue baking for 15 additional minutes until set and lightly browned.
8. Remove from the heat and drizzle the honey on top to serve.

CHAPTER 11

TOP THIS SAUCES AND TOPPINGS

"Barbecue sauce is like a beautiful woman. If it's too sweet it's bound to be hiding something."
—Lyle Lovett

Sauces and toppings add both flair and flavor to your barbecue. In fact, a good barbecue sauce can elevate simple smoked meats to new levels.

Sauces

Warning, there are a few people like the pitmaster's at Kreuz Market in Texas that take their meat so seriously they don't serve sauces. But I always look forward to experimenting with and sampling a variety of sauces.

Good sauces can be sweet, tangy, or hot. Popular ingredients are juices, vinegars and blazing hot chile peppers. Cooking with wine? Just remember to cook out the alcohol first. That reminds me. I need to take this box of wine back to the store and complain. It said once opened, it would last for up to six weeks. Mine only lasted for three days!

You'll find more than a few new sauce favorites in the recipes that follow.

Marinades

Marinades can pull double duty when it comes to preparing your meat. Not only will they add flavor, but marinades also work to tenderize tougher cuts. A tenderizing marinade will need to have an acidic ingredient or natural tenderizing enzyme (like papaya or pineapple). The rest of the magic all depends on the time and the cut of meat. Steaks and larger cuts of beef can marinate for 6 to 24 hours. But fish and seafood only need 15 - 30 minutes.

Marinade Tips

- Use your refrigerator to marinate rather than at room temperature.
- If you plan to baste with the marinade or use it in a sauce, reserve an amount prior to making contact with the meat. You don't want to cross-contaminate or accidentally double dip.
- Pat dry meat after marinating to permit uniform browning and achieve a better crust.

Brines

Salt is at the center of a brine. Different than a marinade (that tenderizes with acidic qualities and enzymes), a brine uses salt and seasonings dissolved in water to make full contact with the food surface in a uniformed concentration. In his book, "Ratios," author Michael Ruhlman describes the definitive ratio or formula for brine as 20 parts water to 1-part salt. This is a 5% salt solution. This "magic" formula has the power to soak flavor into the core fiber of the muscle. But be careful not to over brine, or over salt if you are brining.

Standard Brine:
20 ounces water (2½ cups)
1 ounce kosher salt (2 tablespoons)

Quadrupled:
80 ounces water (10 cups)
4 ounces kosher salt (½ cup)

Combine salt and water and heat until salt is dissolved. Remove from heat and allow to cool. Refrigerate and chill before adding meat or vegetables.

Brining Vessel Tricks:
Use large Ziplock bags for chicken and turkey parts
Use a clean and empty cooler for a whole turkey
Use a large soup pot for a whole or butterflied/spatchcocked chicken
Use "Blue Ice" type ice packs to keep your brining solution chilled without diluting longer brines too large for the refrigerator

Injections

Injections are another way to tenderize and add flavor deep into large cuts of meat. It's very similar to a brine that soaks from the inside out. Brines are most commonly found in poultry, such as Cajun turkey, and competition pork butts, and even beef brisket.

Toppings

I mentioned earlier that hot dogs are my thing. You definitely want special toppings when cooking out hot dogs and burgers. The beauty is that you can keep the cooking part easy (really hot dogs are already cooked) so you can enjoy socializing. Just have fun with a topping bar. If you include everyone's favorites, your guests will appreciate it more than if you were serving filet mignon.

Tricks for Getting Sauced

- **Sauce or marinade?** Use sauces differently than you do marinades. Sauces will add flavor on top of the food. They should complement the food and sometimes add moisture. They should not detract from the dish. Marinades soak into the food and remaining marinades are typically discarded. Marinades add flavor and sometimes tenderize.
- **Cut the fat in your sauces.** You can de-fat a sauce that is too oily by funneling the sauce into an empty wine bottle. Once the fat rises to the top, pour it off.
- **Handle your spoon.** You can use the handle of your sauce pot as a convenient spoon holder. Wedge or insert the end of the spoon handle into the pot's handle or the hole in the handle for easy access.
- **Doctor your sauce.** Store-bought barbecue sauces are found in abundance and often at a price much less then it costs to create with individual ingredients. Take your favorite affordable brand and "doctor" it by adding your own fresh ingredients to create a custom flavor. Hoisin, chili sauce, and Worcestershire are great flavors to add in and make it your own.
- **Hydrated onions.** Make a quick burger topping without the fresh ingredients by rehydrating dried minced onion. The onions can add texture to sauces or add them directly onto burgers for that familiar fast-food flavor found on a Big Mac (sauce) and White Castle burger.
- **No cling trick.** Use a non-stick oil spray to help keep syrup and thick pastes from clinging to the sides of your measuring cup. An initial spray will allow for better measuring and easier cleanup.
- **Fresh squeezed leverage.** Use your tongs as a juicer. Use your long-handled BBQ tongs to squeeze lemons or limes and get more juice than if just squeezing by hand.

TOP THIS RECIPES

Slap Yo Mama BBQ Sauce
Bleu Cheese Cowboy Butter Topping
Savory Mustard Sauce
Jalapeño Salsa
Remoulade Burger Topping
Southern White BBQ Sauce
Hot Vinegar BBQ Sauce
Garlic Quattro Formaggi Topping
Chipotle Honey Glaze
Smoky Sweet Plum Sauce
Pickled Red Onion Relish
Kicked-Up Dipping Sauce

Slap Yo Mama BBQ Sauce

Makes 3 cups   35 minutes   Stove

My wife says she could drink this sauce. But I wouldn't recommend it. Everything in moderation! Try it with pork or chicken.

2 cups ketchup
1 cup water
1 onion, finely diced
½ cup molasses
5 tablespoons sugar
5 tablespoons firmly packed light brown sugar
1 tablespoon Worcestershire sauce
1 tablespoon mustard
Juice of 1 lemon
2 teaspoons liquid smoke
1½ teaspoons freshly ground black pepper
2 garlic cloves, minced

1. In a medium saucepan over medium-high heat on the stovetop, add ketchup, water, onion, molasses, sugar, brown sugar, Worcestershire sauce, mustard, lemon juice, liquid smoke, black pepper, and garlic.
2. Bring the sauce to a boil then reduce the heat to low.
3. Cover and simmer for 30 minutes, stirring occasionally.
4. Remove the saucepan from the heat and strain out any big chunks, or puree the sauce.
5. Serve the sauce hot or cold, and store in an air-tight container in the refrigerator, or pour the sauce into jars for canning or longer storage.

Bleu Cheese Cowboy Butter Topping

Makes 1 cup   5 minutes

If you haven't experimented with flavored herb butters, here is an easy one to dress up your next cookout.

1 cup salted butter, softened
4 ounces Bleu cheese crumbles
¼ cup chopped green onion
1 tablespoon firmly packed light brown sugar
1 teaspoon garlic powder
½ - 1 teaspoon cayenne pepper, depending on desired heat
½ teaspoon onion powder
½ teaspoon freshly ground black pepper

1. In a mixing bowl, cream the butter and Bleu cheese with a mixer.
2. Stir in green onion, brown sugar, garlic powder, cayenne pepper, onion powder, and black pepper.
3. Using wax paper, roll the mixture into a cylindrical log and wrap to seal well.
4. Refrigerate the butter log for a minimum of 4 hours.
5. When ready to serve, unwrap and cut into 1" slices.
6. Serve a slice on steaks or vegetables for a burst of flavor.
7. Wrap tightly and store in the refrigerator for up to 2 weeks.

 Add 4 slices of cooked, crumbled bacon and ½ cup finely chopped pecans to the above for a different flavor combination, or change up the herbs to your favorites!

Savory Mustard Sauce

 Makes 2 cups ⏲ 10 minutes 🔥 Stove

South Carolina barbecue uses mustard as one of its central flavors. Sometimes called "Carolina Gold" for its golden hue, this sauce is the perfect combination of sweet and sour. Different from honey mustard, the apple cider vinegar and ketchup smooth out a little of the mustard bite. I love it.

1 cup mustard
½ cup firmly packed light brown sugar
¼ cup apple cider vinegar
¼ cup ketchup
1 tablespoon Worcestershire sauce
1 teaspoon chipotle chili powder
1 teaspoon garlic powder
1 teaspoon onion powder
1 teaspoon kosher salt
½ teaspoon freshly ground black pepper
½ - 1 teaspoon hot sauce, depending on desired heat

1. In a medium saucepan over medium-high heat on the stovetop, whisk in mustard, brown sugar, apple cider vinegar, ketchup, Worcestershire sauce, chipotle chili powder, garlic powder, onion powder, salt, black pepper, and hot sauce until all dissolved.
2. Reduce heat to low and simmer for 10 minutes. Let cool.
3. Pour into an air-tight container and store in the refrigerator for up to 2 weeks.

Jalapeño Salsa

 Makes 1 cup   🥣 5 minutes

I have only just discovered this creamy and super easy sauce over the last two years. It was one of those "where have you been all my life" moments. The ingredients are amazingly simple. If you haven't been able to tell, I'm a chile head. I love a high level of heat, too. So be wary.

3-5 fresh jalapeños, seeded and cut in half
1/3 cup olive oil
¼ cup chopped fresh cilantro
¼ cup sour cream
2 tablespoons minced garlic
2 teaspoons kosher salt

1. In a blender, add the seeded jalapeños, olive oil, cilantro, sour cream, garlic, and salt.
2. Blend until smooth.
3. If the consistency needs to be thinned out, add 1 tablespoon mayonnaise.
4. Store in an air-tight container in the refrigerator for up to 2 weeks.

Remoulade Burger Topping

Makes 1½ cups   5 minutes

The name is much fancier then the sauce. It just screams big stacked burger and has a very familiar taste. Currently, there is no common mainstream burger sauce like this packaged for sale in stores, so it's always good to make this special sauce at home and serve it to guests along with two all-beef patties, lettuce, cheese, pickles, onions, and a sesame seed bun.

1 cup mayonnaise
1/3 cup creamy French salad dressing
3 tablespoons dill pickle relish
1 tablespoon sweet pickle salad cubes
2 teaspoons apple cider vinegar
2 teaspoons ketchup
2 teaspoons sugar
2 teaspoons dry minced onion
½ teaspoon kosher salt

1. In a small bowl, whisk together mayonnaise, French dressing, dill pickle relish, sweet salad cubes, vinegar, ketchup, sugar, minced onion, and salt.
2. Microwave on high for 30 seconds and stir.
3. Chill 1-2 hours before serving.
4. Store in an air-tight container in the refrigerator for up to 2 weeks.

 To make it into a spicy dip, try adding 1 tablespoon hot sauce and 2 teaspoons Cajun seasoning. Serve with onion rings or fried green tomatoes.

Southern White BBQ Sauce

Makes 2 cups   5 minutes

White barbecue sauce has it's origins in Alabama where it is used to slather on whole chicken pieces. I've come to love it as a wing dipping sauce instead of ranch or blue cheese.

1 cup mayonnaise
½ cup water
¼ cup apple cider vinegar
2 tablespoons sugar
2 teaspoons garlic powder
1 teaspoon dry ground mustard powder
1 teaspoon lemon juice
1 teaspoon horseradish
1 teaspoon kosher salt
1 teaspoon freshly ground black pepper
½ - 1teaspoon cayenne pepper, depending on desired heat

1. In a medium bowl, combine mayonnaise, water, vinegar, sugar, garlic powder, dry ground mustard powder, lemon juice, horseradish, salt, pepper, and cayenne pepper.
2. Mix well, and chill 1-2 hours before serving.
3. Store in an air-tight container in the refrigerator for up to 2 weeks.

 Try using this sauce as a base for Cole slaw.

Hot Vinegar BBQ Sauce

Makes 3 cups   15 minutes   Stove

Most barbecue sauces feature at least some vinegar for tartness. North Carolina style vinegar sauces are primarily vinegar and, thus, can be a bit too much for some people.

Here I thicken it up with ketchup and extra brown sugar for sweetness.

1 cup ketchup
1 cup apple cider vinegar
½ cup firmly packed light brown sugar
4 ounces (½ cup) hot sport peppers in vinegar, pureed
1 tablespoon molasses (or honey)
1 teaspoon kosher salt
1 teaspoon freshly ground black pepper
½ teaspoon ground allspice

1. In a medium saucepan over medium heat on the stovetop, add ketchup, apple cider vinegar, brown sugar, pureed hot sport peppers in vinegar, molasses, salt, pepper, and allspice.
2. Bring to a boil and reduce heat to low.
3. Cover and simmer for 10 minutes until bubbly.
4. Remove from heat and cool.
5. Store in an air-tight container in the refrigerator for up to 2 weeks.

 Hold on to your empty vinegar bottles. They are the perfect size to repurpose and store sauces like this.

Garlic Quattro Formaggi Topping

🍗 Makes 4 cups   🕐 15 minutes   🔥 Stove

Quattro Formaggi literally means "four cheese," which translates to four times the flavor in this creamy cheese sauce topping.

8 ounces cream cheese, softened
½ cup (1 stick) unsalted butter
4 ounces shredded Parmesan cheese
4 ounces Gruyere cheese, grated
4 ounces Asiago cheese, grated (or Romano)
½ cup heavy whipping cream
½ cup half 'n half (or milk)
1 cup chicken broth
1 tablespoon minced garlic
1 teaspoon kosher salt
½ teaspoon freshly ground black pepper

1. Cut the cream cheese block into 1-inch cubes.
2. In a medium saucepan over medium heat on the stovetop, add the butter, cream cheese cubes, Parmesan cheese, Gruyere cheese, Asiago cheese, whipping cream, half 'n half, chicken broth, garlic, salt, and pepper.
3. Heat through, stirring constantly, about 3-4 minutes.
4. Reduce heat to low and cover.
5. Simmer for 5-10 minutes until smooth and slightly thickened.
6. Remove the sauce from the heat and set aside to thicken for about 5 minutes before serving. Note, it will not thicken much before it is removed from the heat.
7. Once the sauce is thicker, drizzle over meat or vegetables, or stir in cooked pasta to serve.

Chipotle Honey Glaze

🔥 Makes 1½ cups 🕐 10 minutes 🔥 Stove

Chipotle peppers are another secret ingredient. They are actually just smoked jalapeño peppers. So, in one little concoction you get smoke and heat. Canned chipotles come in a flavorful sauce that's also great to amp up other sauces. Here, we use dry ground chipotle powder. But don't rule out the canned stuff.

2/3 cup honey
¼ cup water
2 tablespoons tomato paste
1 tablespoon apple cider vinegar
1 teaspoon chipotle chili powder
½ teaspoon onion powder
½ teaspoon salt
½ teaspoon freshly ground black pepper

1. In a small saucepan over medium heat on the stovetop, whisk together honey, water, tomato paste, apple cider vinegar, chipotle chili powder, onion powder, salt, and pepper, stirring constantly.
2. Bring to a boil and immediately reduce the heat to low.
3. Simmer the sauce for 5 minutes and remove from the heat.
4. Let cool. Note, it will thicken as it cools.
5. Serve hot over chicken, pork or vegetables, or use as a marinade.
6. Store in an air-tight container in the refrigerator for up to 2 weeks.

Smoky Sweet Plum Sauce

✒ Makes 2 cups   🕐 25 minutes   🔥 Stove

OK, it's time for me to get judgmental on jelly. I say grape jelly Is way overrated. My favorite jam is plum. It's not quite as easy to find as other preserves but it has just the right depth of flavor to serve as a secret ingredient for a sweet and sticky sauce. Yes, plum. That's my jam.

1 (12-ounce) jar plum jam
2 tablespoons apple cider vinegar
1 tablespoon firmly packed brown sugar
1 tablespoon dry minced onion
1 teaspoon red pepper flakes
2 cloves garlic, minced
½ teaspoon ground ginger
½ - 1 teaspoon kosher salt
½ teaspoon freshly ground black pepper

1. In a medium saucepan over medium-high heat on the stovetop, stir together plum jam, apple cider vinegar, brown sugar, minced onion, red pepper flakes, garlic, ginger, salt, and pepper.
2. Bring the sauce to a boil and reduce the heat to low.
3. Simmer for 20 minutes until all dissolved, and the sauce is hot. Let cool slightly.
4. May be served hot or cold.
5. Store in an air-tight container in the refrigerator for up to 2 weeks.

Pickled Red Onion Relish

🕐 4-6   🕐 5 minutes + marinate 1-4 hours

Pickled onions, peppers, cucumbers and other vegetables have a special place in barbecue. The best joints will usually feature them somewhere on the menu. I really love it when you can find a pickled topping "bar" and you can pick and choose as much as you want.

Be sure to use red onions to naturally add the beautiful red coloring to your plate.

¼ cup rice vinegar
2 tablespoons sesame oil
3 tablespoons pineapple juice
1 teaspoon Dijon mustard
1 teaspoon soy sauce
1 teaspoon garlic powder
½ teaspoon kosher salt
½ teaspoon freshly ground black pepper
1 red onion, sliced thin in a julienne fashion
1 sweet yellow or Vidalia onion, sliced thin in a julienne fashion
1 carrot, sliced thin in a julienne fashion

1. In a small bowl, whisk together rice vinegar, sesame oil, pineapple juice, Dijon mustard, soy sauce, garlic powder, salt, and pepper until well-combined. Set aside.
2. Place the red onion, sweet onion, and carrot into a large bowl and pour the marinade over.
3. Toss to coat well, cover and refrigerate for 1- 4 hours.
4. Serve chilled as a side salad or as a condiment.

Kicked-Up Dipping Sauce

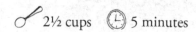 2½ cups   🕐 5 minutes

Add a little zing to your wing, or whatever you're dipping.

2 cups mayonnaise
¼ cup ketchup
1 tablespoon Worcestershire sauce
1 teaspoon hot sauce
1 teaspoon garlic powder
1 teaspoon seasoned salt (Lawry's)
1 teaspoon freshly ground black pepper

1. In a medium bowl, combine mayonnaise, ketchup, Worcestershire sauce, hot sauce, garlic powder, seasoned salt, and pepper, and stir until well-blended.
2. Chill for 1-2 hours before serving.
3. Store in an air-tight container in the refrigerator for up to 2 weeks.

CHAPTER 12

RUBS & PASTES

"Swallow your pride. It has no calories."
—J.W. Post

One of the special things about barbecue is there is so much of it you do with your hands. Good barbecue isn't just cooked up, *it's handcrafted.*

Author and grill master, Steven Raichlen recommends that you always mix spices with your fingers so you can effectively break down any small clumps. Of course, you'll get a better mix, but there's also something therapeutic to it. It's kinda like the grown-up version of playing in the sandbox. It's just fun.

Also, as inferred by a barbecue rub's name, *you rub in these spices with your fingers.* This physically embeds the oils, salt, and flavor into the pores of the food. If you like to work with your hands, then barbecue is the food for you.

Rub Tips

Rubs are a cornerstone of traditional barbecue. The great thing is you can adjust the mix to your liking. Here are a few common variations:

Basic BBQ

Barbecue rubs are a mix of salt, paprika, and sugar. After that, enjoy playing with the flavors and including the heat, or not, of your favorite pepper. The heavier the coating you apply to the meat, the less salt you'll want in the mix. For the most part, big pieces of meat can withstand the use of a lot of salt.

Greek

Greek spices tend to be herbaceous and remind you of the best of the Mediterranean. These seasonings usually include the usual same salt and pepper with extras like oregano, garlic, parsley, and sometimes mint.

Poultry

Poultry seasoning is a standard mixture that won't overpower white meat. Chicken and turkey are commonly seasoned with rubs that include thyme, sage, and rosemary. Don't forget to use your fingers and get under the skin where you can.

Steak

Steak rubs usually include a robust, coarse, salt and pepper blend with dehydrated garlic granulated onion as well as ground coriander. One common brand is a Montreal Steak seasoning. Grill Mates is a brand name of the seasoning by McCormick.

Fish

Seafood rubs can vary from lemon pepper to garlic to my favorite Old Bay. These are typically lighter with less salt to compliment the lighter texture of seafood.

Cajun

Cajun Seasoning also has many variations, but you can count on a bit of heat from cayenne pepper.

Blackening

Blackening spice will be similar to a Cajun seasoning with plenty of pepper applied heavily and cooked onto the surface of the meat to form a tasty thin dark crust.

Spice Warnings

When using rubs for barbecue, keep a few of these warnings top of mind:

First, remember to wash your hands often. If your hands are making contact with the raw meats use extra caution not to touch canisters and other utensils that can cross-contaminate other foods or cooking utensils with bacteria.

Second, remember spices can burn your skin. Use care to avoid touching your eyes, nose, or any "sensitive tissue." Many chefs need to wear rubber gloves.

Lastly, when mixing seasonings, be sure to monitor your salt levels, especially when using already packaged mixes like garlic salt or Cajun seasoning, that already come with salt added.

Rub Tricks

- **Make it stick.** You can use oil or mustard to make your rub stick. I like to use an inexpensive yellow mustard to coat the meat before applying rubs to ribs and butts. It won't add much flavor, but it does help form a better bark.
- **Raise 'em up.** One good practice is to always sprinkle on seasonings from a few inches above the meat, so you get a nice, even coating on the surface. Remember the saying, "higher the better, even spreader!"
- **Texture boost.** Hearty and rustic rubs can enhance your barbecue. Especially with thick-cut steaks and chops where you can indulge in big flavors. Use coarse crystals of sugar like in Sugar in the Raw, sea salt, or chunky dehydrated garlic to help create a true element of surprise for your tongue.
- **Natural cure.** Some pitmasters will include a bit of nitrate-rich curing salt to rubs to enhance the color of the bark and enhance the smoke ring. You can do this naturally by

using ground celery seed, celery powder, or celery salt. Because celery has a high level of nitrates, it is often used as an "all-natural" cure.

- **Check the organics.** Often when I am shopping for spices at the grocery, I fall into analysis paralysis. There are so many options; it's hard to zero in on your best choice. Just remember to explore the entire spice section. If you can't find something specific, check the organics rack for additional options. With so many little jars that all look alike, I've found the pricing, placement, and selection to be erratic. Typically, I wouldn't choose organic spices but don't overlook them if you feel something is missing.

- **Heat your rub.** You can dry roast your spice rubs to bloom them and give them optimal flavor. The added heat will release and activate oils. Roast before mixing with sugar. It's a small step that helps a lot.

- **Freeze your rub.** As outlined in our seasoning tips, you can extend the life of your rubs and seasonings by keeping them cool and in the dark. Storing them in the freezer is much better than over the stove or near direct sunlight. Sunlight and heat over time will degrade flavors.

- **Cool beans.** You can keep finely ground seasonings and spice rubs from clumping with this simple trick. You've probably already noticed dry rice in salt shakers to help with this problem. You can do the same with your seasoning shakers with larger holes. Instead of rice, use dried beans. Not only will the beans absorb the moisture that causes the clumping, but it will also break up the clumps when you shake the canisters.

- **Grind your own.** Freshly ground spice rubs will always have deeper and better flavor than their premixed and packaged counterparts. Grind and mix your own for freshness. An inexpensive coffee grinder or magic bullet blender is a great tool for grinding and blending your own spice mixes. Just clean it thoroughly before grinding coffee beans unless you like garlic pepper cappuccino!

- **Wrap in foil.** If you're using your hands to rub in your seasoning, you'll want to watch what you touch. Try wrapping your spice jars and shakers with a layer of aluminum foil you can easily discard for more sanitary cleanup.

RUBS & PASTES RECIPES

Memphis BBQ Rub
Canadian Blackened Steak Rub
Homemade Chili Powder
Greek All-Purpose Rub
Chinese 5-Spice Blend
Seafood Spice Rub
Caribbean Rub
Tex-Mex Spice Blend
Garlic Pear Seasoning Paste
Sweet Hot Tiger Sauce
Citrus Chile Butter Paste
Dry Chimichurri Rub

Memphis BBQ Rub

🥄 Makes 1¼ cups   🕐 5 minutes

Memphis is one of my favorite cities. From Graceland to the Peabody Hotel there's a lot to discover. It has also become famous for dry rub ribs thanks to Charlie Vergos' famous Rendezvous restaurant. You can find sauced ribs elsewhere in town, but when it comes to dry rub they do it the best.

¼ cup Cajun seasoning
¼ cup smoked paprika
¼ cup sugar
¼ cup firmly packed light brown sugar
1 tablespoon **Homemade Chili Powder** (*found in this chapter*)
1 tablespoon cayenne pepper
1 tablespoon garlic powder
1 tablespoon onion powder
1 teaspoon coriander seeds, crushed
1 teaspoon dry ground mustard

1. In a large bowl, whisk together, or use your fingers to blend the Cajun seasoning, paprika, sugar, brown sugar, chili powder, cayenne pepper, garlic powder, onion powder, crushed coriander seeds, and dry mustard.
2. Great for seasoning ribs, brisket, whole hog, Boston butt, or anything you want to taste good!
3. Store in an air-tight container for up to a month.

Canadian Blackened Steak Rub

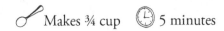 Makes ¾ cup 🕐 5 minutes

This is the ultimate steak rub. Although it is a simple blend, you still have a lot of options to boost texture and flavor. Use coarse ingredients like the dehydrated garlic and fresh black peppercorns and grind these with a mortar and pestle or grinder for the freshest results.

2 tablespoons freshly ground black pepper
2 tablespoons kosher salt
1 tablespoon paprika
1 tablespoon dehydrated garlic
1 tablespoon granulated onion
1 tablespoon dill seed
1 tablespoon crushed red pepper flakes
2 teaspoons ground cumin

1. In a medium bowl, whisk together pepper, salt, paprika, garlic powder, onion powder, dill seed, red pepper flakes, and cumin until well-combined.
2. Sprinkle on steaks, lamb, pork, and chicken.
3. Store in an air-tight container for up to a month.

Homemade Chili Powder

✒ Makes 1 cup   🕐 5 minutes   🔥 Stove

If you have ever tried to compete in a chili cook off you should know that this recipe can give you a competitive edge. The trick to having more vibrant flavor is to have a fresher chili powder. You can shop for pre made blends that may have sat on store shelves for months or you can suck it up and make your own. There's no beating the freshness.

2 ounces whole Ancho chiles (dried Poblano peppers)
2 ounces whole dried Guajillo, Anaheim or Puya (Pulla) chiles
1 ounce whole dried Chile de Arbol
3 tablespoons whole cumin seeds
2 teaspoons whole coriander seeds
2 tablespoons Mexican oregano or oregano
2 tablespoons garlic powder
2 teaspoons smoked paprika
¼ teaspoon ground cloves

1. Remove the stems and seeds from the whole dried Ancho, Guajillo, and Chile de Arbol chiles, and place in a large skillet over medium-high heat on the stovetop.
2. Roast until they start to brown slightly, turning often, about 1-2 minutes.
3. Remove the chiles from the pan and set aside. Reduce heat to medium.
4. Add the whole cumin and coriander seeds to the same pan and return to the heat for 1-3 minutes to toast. Remove when they become fragrant.
5. Let it cool and then use a mortar and pestle or electric blender or coffee grinder to blend up the chiles, cumin, and coriander.
6. In a medium bowl, combine the ground chiles, cumin, coriander, Mexican oregano, garlic powder, smoked paprika, and ground cloves.
7. Packed with flavor, use this whenever a recipe calls for chili powder. Great for winning chili contests, and spicing up just about anything!
8. Store in an air-tight container for up to a month.

 Mix up your own secret blend by experimenting with other dry chile pepper possibilities like: Pasilla (moderate heat and sweet), Ancho (moderate heat and fruity) New Mexico (moderate heat and earthy), Cayenne (very hot), and Chipotle (smokey and sweet).

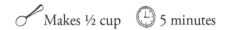

Greek All-Purpose Rub

⌀ Makes ½ cup   🕐 5 minutes

Enjoy the flavors of the Mediterranean with this herbaceous mix that's perfect for most any grilled meat, especially lamb.

3 tablespoons dried oregano
2 teaspoons dried basil
2 teaspoons garlic powder
2 teaspoons onion powder
2 teaspoon smoked paprika
2 teaspoons dried parsley
2 teaspoons freshly ground black pepper
1 teaspoon dried thyme
1 teaspoon ground nutmeg
1 teaspoon ground cinnamon
1 teaspoon kosher salt

1. In a small bowl, whisk together oregano, basil, garlic powder, onion powder, paprika, parsley, black pepper, thyme, nutmeg, cinnamon, and salt. Use your fingers as needed to break up any clumps.
2. Use to season chicken, pork chops, seafood, and vegetables.
3. Store in an air-tight container for up to a month.

 Lemon zest or a garnish of fresh mint is optional.

Chinese 5-Spice Blend

✎ Makes ¼ cup   🕐 5 minutes

You'll feel adventurous when you mix a little Star Anise into your barbecue. Star Anise is actually the fruit of a small evergreen tree and it adds that very distinct licorice taste to chai teas, pumpkin spice flavors as well as this Chinese five spice blend.

2 tablespoons ground star anise
1 tablespoon ground cinnamon
2½ teaspoons ground cloves
1 teaspoon ground fennel seeds
½ teaspoon freshly ground black pepper

1. In a small bowl, whisk together star anise, cinnamon, cloves, fennel, and pepper until well-combined.
2. Use this potent spice sparingly to give meat and vegetable dishes an Asian twist.
3. Store in an air-tight container for up to a month.

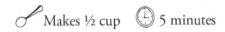

Seafood Spice Rub

Makes ½ cup   ⏱ 5 minutes

This seafood seasoning has just the right amount of punch and heat to compliment your next low country boil. Use more or less cayenne; just be sure to have a cold beer handy either way!

2 tablespoons kosher salt
2 tablespoons celery seed
1 tablespoon ground lemon pepper
1 tablespoon garlic powder
2 teaspoons smoked paprika
2 teaspoons ground ginger
1 teaspoon dry ground mustard
1 teaspoon allspice
1 teaspoon cayenne pepper
1 teaspoon cardamom
1 teaspoon white pepper (or black pepper)

1. In a small bowl, whisk together salt, celery seed, lemon pepper, garlic powder, paprika, ginger, dry mustard, allspice, cayenne pepper, nutmeg, and white pepper.
2. Use to season fish, shrimp, crab, and lobster.
3. Store in an air-tight container for up to a month.

Caribbean Rub

 Makes 1½ cups   🕐 5 minutes

The allspice and brown sugar used here give this spice blend it's signature "jerk" flavor. Feel free to experiments with different sugars like the less processed, larger grain, Demerara, Turbinado, or even Muscovado sugar (also known as Barbados sugar) for even more depth of flavor.

½ cup firmly packed light brown sugar
½ cup smoked paprika
2½ tablespoons ground cinnamon
2 tablespoons ground ginger
1 tablespoon kosher salt
2 teaspoons allspice
2 teaspoons nutmeg
2 teaspoons freshly ground black pepper
1-2 teaspoons cayenne pepper, depending on desired heat

1. In a medium bowl, whisk together brown sugar, paprika, cinnamon, ginger, salt, allspice, nutmeg, black pepper, and cayenne pepper.
2. Use it to season chicken, pork or fish for a Caribbean flair.
3. Store in an air-tight container for up to a month.

Tex-Mex Spice Blend

 Makes ½ cup   🕐 5 minutes

This spice mixture is perfect for your next South of the border meal. The Tex-Mex punch comes from the Mexican oregano. It has a more earthy and intense flavor than typical oregano that some have described as citrusy.

It's also popular in Cuban cuisine.

¼ cup **Homemade Chili Powder** (*found in this chapter*)
2 tablespoons ground cumin
1 tablespoon kosher salt
1 tablespoon freshly ground black pepper
2 teaspoons smoked paprika
1 teaspoon garlic powder
1 teaspoon onion powder
1 teaspoon Mexican oregano
1 teaspoon crushed red pepper flakes

1. In a medium bowl, combine Homemade Chili Powder, cumin, salt, pepper, paprika, garlic powder, onion powder, oregano, and crushed red pepper flakes.
2. Great for tacos, enchiladas, fajitas, and quesadillas.
3. Store in an air-tight container for up to a month.

Garlic Pear Seasoning Paste

⏲ Makes 1½ cups 🕐 10 minutes

Fresh pears add a light sweetness to this light summer time seasoning paste. Perfect for summer, but great any time of year when you can find fresh pears. Remove any seeds that will add bitterness to the blend.

1 onion, cut into quarters
12 cloves garlic, peeled
4 pears, peeled and cut into large chunks
1 ounce (¼ cup) fresh ginger, peeled and cut into chunks
¼ cup olive oil
2 tablespoons apple cider vinegar

1. Using a blender, add the onion quarters, garlic cloves, pear chunks, ginger chunks, olive oil, and apple cider vinegar.
2. Blend until smooth.
3. Use to baste or marinate meat for a sweet Asian flavor.
4. Store in an air-tight container in the refrigerator for up to 2 weeks.

Sweet Hot Tiger Sauce

🕐 Makes 3 cups   🕐 10 minutes

Shout out to Joe Exotic. At the time of this writing Tiger King is sweeping the nation. Rest assured no big cats were harmed in the making of this zesty sauce.

½ cup **Fridge Pickles & Peppers** (*found in **Nuts, Cheese, Desserts & More***), drained
½ cup Ponzu
½ cup firmly packed light brown sugar
1 (8-ounce) can tomato sauce (reserve remaining tomato sauce for another use)
¼ cup **Slap Yo Mama BBQ Sauce** (*found in **Top This***)
2 tablespoons red wine vinegar
1 teaspoon crushed red pepper flakes
½-1 teaspoon hot sauce, depending on desired heat
1 teaspoon garlic powder

1. Using a food processor or a blender, add Fridge Pickles & Peppers, and Ponzu, and puree until smooth.
2. In a medium bowl, add the pureed pickles and peppers.
3. Whisk in the brown sugar, tomato sauce, Slap Yo Mama BBQ Sauce, red wine vinegar, red pepper flakes, hot sauce, and garlic powder, until well-combined.
4. Use as a marinade or dressing for all meats.
5. Store in an air-tight container in the refrigerator for up to 2 weeks.

 Ponzu is a sweet and sour, citrus seasoned soy sauce found in the grocery aisle with Asian foods. It's similar to teriyaki sauce, but not as sweet, with a tart flavor added.

Citrus Chile Butter Paste

Makes 2 cups   5 minutes

Compound butters and blends like this add a rich layer of flavor to all sorts of grilled foods. The citrus zest used here makes it a top choice for fresh grilled seafood.

1 cup (2 sticks) unsalted butter, softened to room temperature
¼ cup chipotle chiles in adobo sauce
Zest of 1 lime
1 teaspoon minced garlic
1 teaspoon dried cilantro
½ teaspoon kosher salt

1. Using a food processor, add butter, chipotle chiles in adobo sauce, lime zest, garlic, cilantro, and salt, and pulse until smooth and blended.
2. Use at room temperature to season seafood, chicken, steaks, corn, and other vegetables for a spicy citrus flavor.
3. Place the butter into an air-tight container and store in the refrigerator for up to 2 weeks.

Dry Chimichurri Rub

🧂 Makes 1 cup   🕐 5 minutes

Chimichurri is a sauce which originated in the countryside of Argentina and Uruguay that brings great flavor to beef. This recipe is an herbaceous dry rub blend, rather than the usual sauce. Using fresh herbs would enhance the flavors, but it would need to be stored in the refrigerator and only keep for a few days, so we have used dry spices here.

3 tablespoons dried basil
2 tablespoons dried cilantro
2 tablespoons dried parsley
1 tablespoon dried oregano
1 tablespoon smoked paprika
1 tablespoon garlic powder
1 tablespoon kosher salt
1 tablespoon freshly ground black pepper
2 teaspoons crushed red pepper flakes
2 teaspoons dry minced onion

1. In a small bowl, whisk together basil, cilantro, parsley, oregano, paprika, garlic, salt, pepper, red pepper flakes, and dry minced onion.
2. Use this to season steaks, chicken, salmon, and shrimp.
3. To make this into a chimichurri finishing sauce, add Dry Chimichurri Rub to a medium bowl and stir in ½ cup olive oil, ¼ cup red wine vinegar, and the juice of one lemon. Stir to combine.

ABOUT THE AUTHOR

BILL WEST is a country music authority, barbecue enthusiast, and bestselling multi-cookbook author based in Charleston, South Carolina. He has been the on-air host and operations manager of Charleston's leading radio stations, and has interviewed some of entertainment's biggest celebrities, including Taylor Swift, Darius Rucker, Paula Deen, Zac Brown, Ryan Seacrest, Brad Paisley, Garth Brooks, Keith Urban, Carrie Underwood, and Alton Brown, to name a few.

His blog at BarbecueTricks.com and his YouTube channel have accumulated more than 10 million views and 40,000+ subscribers. A native of Glenview, Illinois, West is the youngest of six children and has spent the last 30 years in the Southeast playing country music on the radio. Certified pitmasters, he and his wife, MJ, competed in and judged barbecue competitions across the state for several years before Bill took up writing. Armed with a degree in broadcast journalism from Bradley University in Peoria, Illinois, he took his first "real job" in sunny Hilton Head Island, South Carolina, in 1989 (just one week before Hurricane Hugo).

Bill and MJ make their home in Charleston, South Carolina, and have one son, Jack, who is a gifted fingerstyle guitar player, on track to becoming the next Chet Atkins…or Brad Paisley.

Download Bill's free *Sides & Sauces* eBook: BarbecueTricks.com/sauces-sides-recipes
Get his book *BBQ Blueprint* here: BarbecueTricks.com/the-bbq-blueprint
Get his book *The Complete Electric Smoker Cookbook* here:
BarbecueTricks.com/electric-smoker-cookbook
Get his book *The Ultimate Wood Pellet Smoker Grill Cookbook* here: BarbecueTricks.com/
wood-pellet-grill-smoker-book/
Get his book *Smoking Meat 101* here: BarbecueTricks.com/smoking-meat-101/

Follow Bill West:
twitter.com/BarbecueTricks
facebook.com/BarbecueTricks

RESOURCES

Many of the documents in this book are available as free
downloads in high resolution on our website
https://BarbecueTricks.com
http://barbecuetricks.com/book-resources

If there are updated versions of this book, we will notify you if you join our community at
https://barbecuetricks.com/free-newsletter

Much of the material in this book has been produced in instructional video form.
Subscribe to the YouTube Channel at
https://www.youtube.com/user/BarbecueTricks

Facebook - https://www.facebook.com/BarbecueTricks

ONE LAST THING...

I don't want you to head off into the wild world of BBQ without me saying one more "Thank You" for buying this book. I know there are a lot of cookbooks out there on grilling, and you took a chance on this one.

I hope you also take advantage of picking up my Barbecue Sides and Sauces book for FREE as my gift to you. Get it here: https://barbecuetricks.com/sauces-sides-recipes

Finally, if you liked what you've read, then I need your help. Please take a moment to leave a review for this book on Amazon. I'll read them all, and it will not only help me know what you like but it also really helps spread the word on Amazon. Even a very short note is very appreciated.

CPSIA information can be obtained
at www.ICGtesting.com
Printed in the USA
LVHW022144111220
673921LV00010B/601

9 781735 665634